CW00524373

City Technology College

City Technology College

Geoffrey Walford
and
Henry Miller

Open University Press
Milton Keynes • Philadelphia

Open University Press
Celtic Court
22 Ballmoor
Buckingham
MK18 1XW

and

1900 Frost Road, Suite 101
Bristol, PA 19007, USA

First Published 1991

British Library Cataloguing in Publication Data

Walford, Geoffrey
  City Technology College.
  1. Great Britain. Secondary education
  I. Title
  373.2410941

  ISBN 0-335-09275-6

Library of Congress Cataloging-in-Publication Data

Walford, Geoffrey.
    City technology college/Geoffrey Walford, Henry Miller.
      p.   cm.
    Includes bibliographical references (p.   ) and index.
    ISBN 0-335-09275-6
    1. Technical education—Great Britain.   I. Miller, Henry, 1940–
    . II. Title.
  T107.W26   1991
  607.1′141—dc20   90-27370
                                                                CIP

Typeset by Inforum Typesetting, Portsmouth
Printed and bound in Great Britain by Woolnough Bookbinding Ltd,
Irthlingborough, Northamptonshire

Contents

Introduction

In October 1986 the Conservative government in the UK announced that it was to establish a pilot network of twenty new secondary schools to be called City Technology Colleges (CTCs). These were to be a revolutionary new type of school, independent of local education authorities, and funded jointly by sponsors from industry and the Department of Education and Science. They were to select appropriate children for the highly technological curriculum on offer from within a catchment area containing some five or six thousand secondary age children.

In one swoop the CTCs were thus an attack on local education authorities, on comprehensive education, on other schools within the designated catchment areas and on traditional state-maintained education as it had developed over the previous forty years. The CTC concept was born in controversy and, in consequence, the colleges have remained in the media headlines.

Unfortunately much of the debate about City Technology Colleges has been conducted in ignorance, for few people know what they are actually like and what their effect on nearby local authority schools has been. This book sheds some light on these issues. It reports the results of a research study of the first City Technology College, Kingshurst, which opened in Solihull in September 1988. It describes and discusses the way in which that college has developed – its staff, students, selection procedures, curriculum, facilities, teaching methods and ethos. Then it looks at the reactions and responses from the local schools and community to the presence of the CTC.

In gathering research data we interviewed local industrialists, politicians, local authority administrators, Headteachers and teachers within Birmingham and Solihull. The Heads and teachers of neighbouring schools were particularly helpful in giving us access to their schools, providing us with information, and allowing us to interview pupils.

The chapters on the City Technology College itself are based on ethnographic research conducted during the autumn term of 1989. During that time lessons were observed, teachers and pupils interviewed, pupil questionnaires completed and a vast quantity of other information gained through participant observation.

We wish to thank all those people who have made this research possible. We are particularly indebted to Mrs Valerie Bragg, Principal of Kingshurst CTC, and the staff and students of the college, for allowing one of us to enter into their world and experience their kindness and hospitality. Although this book could not have been written without their generous help, it is far from being uncritical of CTCs, and the responsibility for the descriptions and arguments put forward here is ours alone.

The Kingshurst case study was funded by the Strategic Innovation Research Group at Aston University, and through a consultancy to an ESRC-funded research project on City Technology Colleges directed by Professors Tony Edwards and Geoff Whitty (Grant no. C00232462).

Chapters 1, 3, 4, 5 and 6 were written by Geoffrey Walford and chapters 2, 7 and 8 were jointly written by Geoffrey Walford and Henry Miller.

1

The national plan

On 7 October 1986 the then Secretary of State for Education and Science, Kenneth Baker, announced the creation of a pilot network of twenty City Technology Colleges to be jointly funded by central government and industrial sponsors. Mr Baker, who had replaced Sir Keith Joseph in May 1986, chose the Conservative Party Annual Conference which preceded the 1987 general election to break the news officially of the new City Technology Colleges. He did so to an enthusiastic hand-picked audience. The initiative was explicitly presented as one of a number of new measures intended to 'break the grip' of left-wing education authorities and one designed to offer new hope and opportunity to selected young people and parents. As the name suggests, City Technology Colleges were to be created to provide a curriculum rich in science and technology, but they were also designed for a specific group of 11–18 year olds from the inner city. They were to be independent schools, run by educational trusts with close links to industry, but directly government funded in line with *per capita* local authority funding for schools in similar areas. They were to charge no fees, and sponsors were expected to meet a substantial part of the costs of the buildings and equipment necessary to provide a highly technological curriculum.

Further details of the plan were given in a glossy brochure published by the Department of Education and Science a week after the speech (DES 1986), which was sent to about 2,000 leading industrial and commercial organizations asking them to support the new venture. According to that booklet, it was in the cities that the education system was under the most pressure and where the government's aims and parents' aspirations 'often seem furthest from fulfilment'.

> There are many examples of good schooling offered by committed teachers in the cities. But many families living there who seek the best possible education for their children do not have access to the kind of schools which measure up to their ambitions.
>
> The government believes that there is, in the business community and elsewhere, a widespread wish to help extend the range of choice for families in urban areas.
>
> (DES 1986: 3)

The City Technology College initiative was thus firmly linked to the idea of widening and improving educational provision in urban areas, particularly the disadvantaged inner cities, where the government seemed to believe that the local authority education system was often failing children. Some of the areas to be chosen for a CTC were to be those 'suffering acute social deprivation and receiving attention in other ways through the Inner City Initiative', which the government had previously established. Within the DES booklet a map was provided showing twenty-six possible locations, including eight which were already included in Inner City Initiatives. These eight were Handsworth in Birmingham; Chapeltown, Leeds; St Paul's, Bristol; Moss Side, Manchester; Highfields, Leicester; Notting Hill and North Peckham in London, and Middlesbrough, North Central. The attack on the Labour councils which controlled practically all of the inner-city local authorities was not made explicitly in the booklet, but was plain from various political speeches of the time. The City Technology Colleges were thus conceived within the political arena, and have remained entangled within political controversy.

It was planned that each CTC would serve a substantial catchment area, with the composition of the student intake being representative of the community served. These catchment areas were to be defined in such a way that places would be offered to about one in five or six children from within each area. It was made explicit that CTCs would not be academically selective and would be required, as a condition of the grant, to aim at admitting pupils spanning the full range of ability represented in the catchment area. However, selection was still to be a strong feature of the

CTCs. They were not to be 'neighbourhood schools taking all comers', but the Head and governing body were to select applicants on the basis of

> general aptitude, for example as reflected in their progress and achievements in primary school; on their readiness to take advantage of the type of education offered in CTCs; and on their parents' commitment to full-time education or training up to the age of 18, to the distinctive characteristics of the CTC curriculum, and to the ethos of the CTC.
>
> (DES 1986: 5)

Academic selectivity, which might have acted as a vote-loser in the soon expected next general election, was to be replaced by selectivity on a broad range of less easily measurable criteria which would include parents' characteristics as well as those of their children.

There were several other features of the planned colleges that made them exceptional. For example, there was to be a strong emphasis on pupil self-discipline and positive attitudes. The school day and term were likely to be longer than in maintained schools. All pupils were expected to honour the requirements of homework and to participate in extra-curricular activities including residential field trips with physical as well as intellectual challenges. The curriculum was to include a strong technical and practical element within a broad and balanced curriculum for all students up to the age of 16. Work experience was to be an integral part of the curriculum.

As the CTCs were to be private schools, a further major difference between them and local education authority (LEA) schools was that staff were to be employed directly by their governing bodies, who would be free to decide their own pay and conditions of service. Government funding for current expenditure would be based on salaries in maintained schools and staff/student ratios for similar secondary schools, but CTCs would be free to use sponsorship money to improve salaries. Presumably they could also decide to pay some staff less than obtainable in a maintained school. Further flexibility was to be encouraged by allowing governing bodies to decide on the balance between teaching and non-teaching staff and, exceptionally, to employ teaching staff without qualified teacher status.

It is important to recognize that, at the time that the CTC

plan was revealed, nothing was publicly known about the government's later proposals for grant-maintained schools or for the compulsory introduction of local management of schools for LEA schools. All but the smallest LEA schools now have the ability to make major choices about how to use their capitation grant, and grant-maintained schools have been able to detach themselves from their LEAs altogether, but these plans were not made known until May 1987 and were clearly influenced by the government's early experience with CTCs.

The antecedents to City Technology Colleges

In order to understand some of the controversy that the CTC announcement aroused, it is necessary to sketch in briefly some of the educational and political background, and some of the diversity of aims and objectives which can be seen to have influenced the nature of the initiative. Of particular significance is the gradual rise to prominence and legitimacy of the New Right in education over the 1970s and 1980s.

The philosophical stance of the educational New Right is complex and contradictory (Quicke 1988), but the major component is a neo-liberalism which prioritizes the limitation of government in the interests of the liberty of the individual and a free society. Private enterprise is seen as more efficient, effective and desirable than anything provided or organized by government, and since 1979 a policy of privatization has been implemented in areas as diverse as communications, transport, energy and social services (Walford 1990a).

Within education, the New Right has gradually risen to dominate government thinking following the publication of the first of the Black Papers more than two decades ago. This series of critiques of state-maintained education (Cox and Dyson 1971; Cox and Boyson 1975; 1977) attacked various aspects of education policy, but 'progressivism' and the perceived decline of academic standards were the most prominent concerns. The various contributors to the Black Papers did not have identical visions of what was desirable for the future, but they coalesced around a general belief in the inevitability of a hierarchical society, with inequalities in income, wealth and resources, to a large extent linked to differing levels of individual intelligence and ability. Most of the contributors believed in the necessity for selection of children for different schools, the fundamental worth of a grammar school education, and the failure of comprehensive schools to offer an adequate education to children of high ability. Comprehensive schools, especially those in inner-city areas, were largely seen as failing to provide a 'rigorous education' for able working-class pupils. The Black Paper writers argued that removing the meritocratic 'ladder of opportunity' for able working-class children to attend separate grammar schools was a betrayal of the rights of such children and had resulted in a lowering of standards.

In the late 1960s and early 1970s the Black Paper criticisms and policies for change had been ignored or regarded with derision by most educationists but, as the 1980s approached, these ideas began to be treated with considerable seriousness by many Conservative politicians. The advent of the Thatcher Conservative government in 1979, which sought to 'roll back the frontiers of the state' and which was more concerned with individual achievement and advantage than the needs of society as a whole, made the calls from the New Right educational writers more respectable, and policies derived from their ideas were rapidly implemented.

The earliest of these policies, which is now often seen as a precursor to the more recent New Right ideas implemented in the 1988 Education Reform Act, was the Assisted Places Scheme (APS). There are a number of direct similarities between APS and the City Technology College proposals, but Edwards *et al.* (1989; 1991) have shown that the pressure for APS came from more liberal elements from within the private schools sector. The scheme was constructed by Conservative politicians and representatives of ex-direct grant and other private schools during Labour's period in power from 1974 to 1979 and was swiftly put into place through the 1980 Education Act. It was designed to give financial assistance with school fees and other incidental expenses to parents with low incomes who wished to send their children to private schools, and whose children were selected to attend. Parents are means tested and fees remitted according to a sliding scale, with the schools being reimbursed by central government. The scheme was designed to reintroduce the direct grant principle which had existed until 1975, but without the politically indefensible aspect of giving financial support to parents who could already afford to pay.

According to Mark Carlisle, who was Secretary of State for Education and Science when the Assisted Places Scheme was announced in 1980, the aim of the scheme was – 'to give certain children a greater opportunity to pursue a particular form of academic education that was regrettably not otherwise, particularly in cities, available to them' (quoted in Griggs 1985: 89). The Secretary of State thus publicly accepted some of the ideas of the Black Paper writers in suggesting that the private sector was 'better' than the maintained sector, and that the maintained sector (for which he was ultimately responsible), especially in cities, was of insufficient quality to ensure academic success. The proposed solution to this problem was not to try to improve education in all schools where there was perceived to be a need, but to select out only a limited number of children from amongst those who specifically applied for special treatment and offer them the facilities thought to be necessary. The Assisted Places Scheme thus re-legitimized selection and inequality of provision, and encouraged parents to believe that private provision was automatically 'better' than provision in the maintained sector (Walford 1987a). The parallels with the City Technology College concept are obvious.

That there are these similarities between the Assisted Places Scheme and the City Technology Colleges is not coincidental. Although the details of the CTC plan were the responsibility of Kenneth Baker, the original idea for establishing such colleges derived from Sir Keith Joseph's period of office and even earlier. Of particular importance were the ideas of Stuart Sexton who, as educational adviser to Sir Keith and to the previous Secretary of State, Mark Carlisle, had been the major advocate of the Assisted Places Scheme. Edwards et al. (1989) show that Stuart Sexton had worked to try to introduce an assisted places scheme which was far wider than that which eventually emerged. Sexton had been a long-standing supporter of selective education, grammar schools and of a fully privatized and differentiated educational system (Sexton 1977). During the late 1970s he had tried to develop a scheme which would enlarge the private sector by encouraging voluntary aided grammar schools to become private schools receiving some support through an assisted places scheme. He had also wished a far greater proportion of existing private schools to receive assisted places. In the event, political and economic pressures on the new government meant that the Assisted Places Scheme adopted was more limited than Sexton wished, but his desire (and the desire of others on the political right) for a fully privatized educational system supported by vouchers remained unchanged (Sexton 1987).

As the 1980s progressed, the calls from the political right for greater selection and differentiation between schools gradually became more generally acceptable and were linked to a broad desire for increased privatization and greater 'choice in education' (Walford 1990b). The large number of different voices calling for change makes it impossible to state which had the greatest formative influence leading to the CTC initiative. For example, in an Institute of Economic Affairs publication, Dennison (1984) called for more grammar schools, an extension of the Assisted Places Scheme, and the establishment of new private schools. He recommended that new independent schools might be encouraged by handing over the premises of schools to be closed, or by the provision of capital grants. He also suggested the introduction of genuine subsidies to private schools to cover such items as salaries or capital expenditure (Walford 1990a). The *No Turning Back* group of Conservative MPs (Brown *et al.* 1985; 1986) suggested that parents and teachers should be able to start their own schools funded by central government, and encouraged a diversity of specialist schools. Caroline Cox (1985) proposed the development of magnet schools on the US model. These writers and others influenced government advisers who in turn suggested, first, direct grant primary schools and, later, a network of directly funded Crown schools for inner-city areas.

While the privatization issue was of considerable importance, the CTC idea also drew on another very different strand of thought. Much of the debate about selection had been in terms of the perceived needs of more able children, but the CTC idea was linked to concerns about technical and vocational education and training for the average and less academically able children. Here, it was argued that children of high ability were relatively well catered for, but that others were not being provided with the more vocationally orientated curriculum that might better serve their own and the nation's needs. Such attempts to link the educational system more closely to the perceived needs of industry for a well-skilled, motivated and disciplined workforce are far from new (Davies 1986). Although the argument has ebbed and flowed over time, Reeder (1979) has shown that criticism from industrialists about schooling has intensified at times of economic underperformance and decline, as industry searches for a scapegoat for its own failure. It was thus to be expected that such arguments would gain increased prominence in the late 1970s and early 1980s. It is

certainly true that international comparisons show that the proportion of students staying in education beyond the compulsory
school leaving age is far smaller in Britain than in most other
Western countries, and the main reason for this is that most
average and below-average students leave full-time education as
quickly as possible. Those who do continue with full-time education are predominantly those with high academic ability.

City Technology Colleges were thus in part proposed as a
'programme which builds upon the lessons of the Technical and
Vocational Education Initiative (TVEI) and of successful secondary
schools generally' (DES 1986: 3). TVEI had been launched in 1982
as a well-funded pilot project with the aim of incorporating a
technical and vocational element into the curriculum of 14–18
year old pupils. In order to encourage rapid change, it was funded
through the then Manpower Services Commission (now the
Training Agency), and was the responsibility of the Department of
Employment rather than the Department of Education and Science. At that time, the then Trade and Industry Minister, Norman
Tebbit, had suggested that if the local education authorities did not
accept the idea then he would have to set up his own technology
schools. However, as TVEI was initially well funded, the LEAs
were persuaded to enter the scheme – at first reluctantly and later
with enthusiasm. TVEI was quickly expanded until, by 1986, all
local education authorities were taking part – although at much
reduced *per capita* funding. It will be shown in Chapter 2 that some
TVEI projects were successful and had a significant effect on the
relationships between schools and industry at the local level.

TVEI was one way by which the perceived need for more
students to follow technologically and vocationally oriented
courses might be achieved. Specific students within comprehensive
schools were selected to receive a curriculum with a greater emphasis on technology, business and work preparation. The alternative, of course, was to select these children out of the
comprehensive schools altogether and allocate them to separate
schools which would provide the necessary curriculum and facilities. This suggestion was made in January 1986 when the Centre for
Policy Studies held a conference on employment at the House of
Lords attended by fifty leading industrialists, the Prime Minister
and others. It was recognized that many LEAs would be hostile
towards setting up specialist schools and would see this as an attack
on comprehensive education, so it was proposed that the

government should create 100 centrally funded direct-grant technical schools. The report of the conference is given in a booklet
written by Mr (now Sir) Cyril Taylor (1986), former deputy leader
of the Conservative group on the Greater London Council, whose
name recurs. Interestingly, even at this stage, the idea was that these
technical schools should initially be concentrated in deprived inner-
city areas, but that ultimately each of the LEAs should have at least
one technical school 'to serve as a beacon to other schools in the
area' (Taylor 1986: 30). A key internal DES paper on the idea was
prepared by Robert Dunn MP, Minister of State, in February 1986
(Regan 1990: 20) while Keith Joseph was still Secretary of State.

The government's reluctance to support such new forms of
schooling most probably stemmed from the need for further expenditure that they would require. New technology, in particular,
is very expensive and necessitates continual expenditure to keep up
with change. The City Technology College idea is based on the
recognition that additional funding for technological areas in
schools might be available from the industrial and commercial
organizations which it was hoped would eventually benefit from
better-trained recruits. If industry and commerce could be persuaded to support new private technological schools the costs of
the whole initiative would be much reduced, and automatically
there would be firmer links between the schools and industry. In
other private schools funding is mostly from parents in the form of
fees; in CTCs the aim was to tap another potential source of
private funding by allowing industry to sponsor schools.

Stuart Sexton did not become Keith Baker's education adviser,
but is still highly active in promoting New Right policies in education. He is currently Director of the Institute for Economic Affairs
Education Unit and runs his own private technological primary
school. Sexton sees the establishment of new independent CTCs as a
first stage towards a far wider direct grant scheme and as a part of a
'step by step approach to the eventual introduction of a "market
system", of a system truly based upon the supremacy of parental
choice, the supremacy of purchasing power' (Sexton 1987: 11).

Reactions to the CTC plan

Reactions to the proposed City Technology Colleges were swift
and predominantly hostile. Within a few days of the announcement

most of the organizations with an interest in education had voiced objections to the plan, and many of the points made then were to remain at the top of the political debate in the years to come. For example, the general secretary of the National Union of Teachers immediately claimed that it was 'totally irrelevant to the wishes of British parents and to the needs of their children', while the general secretary of the National Association of Head Teachers argued that there was an urgent need for *all* secondary schools to have more technologically based teaching, not just for what would become the privileged few in the inner cities (Carvel and Boseley 1986). As the weeks passed the Secondary Heads Association called for Mr Baker to rethink a proposal 'which would do nothing to further the overall aims of the country for an education system which prepares young people for tomorrow's world'. The Labour Party was absolutely against the idea and Jack Straw, Shadow Secretary of State for Education and Science, has made opposition to CTCs one of his long-running crusades – sometimes with major and politically embarrassing successes.

Objections from these sources must have been expected by government, as was the general opposition of the Association of Metropolitan Authorities (AMA), which at that point represented the thirty-six metropolitan district councils, thirty-one London boroughs, the City of London and the Inner London Education Authority. The AMA thus represented the LEAs into which the majority of CTCs could be expected to be placed and was heavily Labour dominated. The document it produced in February 1987, *City Technology Colleges: A Speculative Investment* (AMA 1987), was a well-considered and argued case against CTCs which analysed the CTC proposals in the light of local authority good practice.

It is worth considering in detail some of the main arguments put forward by the Association of Metropolitan Authorities, for they were frequently repeated by other critics. Any study of CTCs should attempt to test the truth of some of these adverse predictions, and many of them will be considered in later chapters in the light of evidence gained from this case study. The first concern of the AMA was with the perceived departure of the CTC proposals from the principles of the 1944 Education Act, which gave local authorities the responsibility for determining educational provision for their areas, in favour of direct intervention by the Secretary of State. Later legislation introducing grant-maintained schools showed that AMA was undoubtedly correct in expressing its concern about this issue, although it is unlikely that it would have advocated that the 1944 Act be superseded to deal with the anomaly!

The AMA's second concern about the CTCs focused on the potential damage to other schools in the neighbourhoods, and to the effect that a CTC might have on an LEA's ability to reorganize its educational services to deal with falling school rolls. The AMA (1987) stated that most of the authorities designated as possible sites for a CTC had undergone, or were at that time undergoing, re-organization to remove surplus places. Such reorganization requires detailed planning and consultation between the LEA, parents and denominational interests, and AMA argued that the introduction of a new CTC would disrupt this careful planning. The document gives details of five separate examples of unnamed authorities where a CTC would badly damage plans. This disruption not only would be damaging in itself, but also would involve the LEA in further expenditure.

The AMA booklet makes considerable play of the lack of knowledge of local problems and policies that this centrally planned CTC initiative indicates. It gives the example of West Yorkshire, for which a CTC was proposed, which has a middle school system which would make any integration of an 11–18 CTC into existing provision extremely difficult.

A further potential danger seen by AMA was that CTCs might 'cream off' the brighter pupils from neighbouring schools, thus reducing these comprehensive schools to secondary moderns. It argued that selection based on work done in primary schools, and on parental commitment to full-time education after 16, presents particular difficulties, and that the implication that about 80 per cent of pupils within the catchment area will lack the aptitude to study business and technological education was damaging to those other pupils.

A further concern of AMA was that of teacher supply. At that time, as now, there was mounting worry about the supply of teachers in subjects such as mathematics, computer studies, physics, and craft, design and technology (CDT). The AMA argued that the creation of twenty new schools which would specialize in just those subject areas would exacerbate the problems. It was thought that they would both attract a disproportionate number of those teachers from the total national supply and produce local areas of special shortage around each CTC.

The AMA also claimed that the DES had under-estimated the progress that had already occurred in the technological and scientific curriculum in local authority schools in many of the areas designated for CTCs. The booklet gives numerous examples of links between schools and industry and of curriculum innovations. It describes the curriculum already offered in one authority's schools for first to third years and compares this directly with the curriculum suggested for a CTC. The only major difference is shown to be the explicitly separate treatment of Business Understanding in the CTC curriculum proposed by the DES. It describes many TVEI projects in local authority schools which had developed industrial links and provided work experience for pupils, and argued that these links might be endangered by the CTC proposals. The booklet lists the variety of forms of certification already offered for these new courses through the Business and Technician Education Council (BTEC), City & Guilds, A level and other bodies.

Writing in early 1987, the AMA had the benefit of observing the initial reactions of potential sponsors to the CTC programme. The booklet points out that the investment expected of sponsors is very large. Start-up costs were expected to be particularly high (several million pounds per school), and there would be a need for a sustained level of continuing and substantial funding as well.

The AMA response concludes by lamenting

the ill-thought-out nature of the CTC proposals, and the apparent interest in specious remedies for the problems of the Education Service. We would prefer to engage in constructive discussion with the DES on how education in our cities can develop. We have highlighted good practice, which we know to be widespread. The CTCs are not relevant to the needs of the cities: we see that they could do great damage and waste public money . . .

(AMA 1987: 18)

Most of these criticisms could be dismissed by the government as being the bleatings of the 'educational business' – a business which Kenneth Baker argued was dominated by the suppliers rather than the customers or consumers. More unexpected, and more difficult to dismiss, were the criticisms from industry and commerce, the very constituency which the CTCs were designed to please.

In the weeks following Mr Baker's announcement at the Conservative Party Annual Conference in 1986 it became clear that very little groundwork had been done to ensure the success of the CTC proposals. The DES booklet published a few days after the announcement stated that 'The government believes that there is, in the business community and elsewhere, a widespread wish to help extend the range of choice for families in urban areas' (DES 1986: 3). In the months following, however, it became evident that the government had done virtually nothing to see whether their belief was correct or whether the strength of the business community's 'wish to help extend the range of choice' was sufficient actually to support CTCs. Not only had the educational establishment not been consulted on the proposals, but also it seemed that business and industry had been left equally in the dark.

Industrial and commercial organizations were understandably slow in voicing their views about the CTC initiative. CTCs were presented as building on the work of TVEI which very many business organizations were actively supporting, and it might have seemed somewhat churlish to express doubts about this new idea. However, it was the very success of TVEI and related initiatives that caused potential sponsors to question the need for CTCs. Those from industry and commerce recognized that over the previous decade or so there had been a great increase in the links between industry and individual schools. By the mid-1980s there was a plethora of teacher secondment schemes, industrial visits, work-experience placements and so on. TVEI had brought teachers and students into the world of business and industrialists and business people into the schools. Industrial organizations were providing personnel for teaching and course development, were funding a variety of curriculum developments and were providing direct financial help for other specific projects. In short, throughout much of the state-maintained system, there had been a major reorientation of education and training with a shift towards the new vocationalism and closer links between schools and industry (Walford et al. 1988). Given that this had occurred in very many maintained secondary and primary schools, there was little reason why the companies involved should wish to concentrate their attention on CTCs rather than continuing to spread their efforts over a far wider number of schools. Indeed, there was every good reason for them wishing to continue to influence the bulk of mainstream schooling, where the financial and other investment was likely to be smaller and the effect proportionally greater.

As the months passed many of the major industrial and

commercial businesses from whom the government might have expected support declined to become CTC sponsors. For example, in December 1986 the education liaison manager of BP, a company heavily involved with developments in education, made clear his distaste for the CTC scheme at an Industrial Society meeting, and accused the Secretary of State of an unjustified lack of confidence in the majority of schools to deliver the kind of education he was seeking. This representative of BP saw the CTCs as potentially damaging to the rest of the education system. This was followed by a similar claim from the education liaison officer for ICI, and later the then managing director, Sir John Harvey-Jones, who argued that cash for educational projects was finite and that supporting a CTC would inevitably mean that other existing projects developed in association with LEAs would have to be cut. ICI was not prepared to damage the good relationships that they had built with LEAs over the years to support the scheme.

Development of the national scheme: change and uncertainty

The original timetable for the CTC initiative was that the twenty pilot colleges were all to be in operation by 1990, but it gradually beame evident to everyone involved that this was unrealistic. The main problems stemmed from the unwillingness of industry to support new colleges on the scale envisaged for CTCs, the difficulty in obtaining suitable sites within inner-city urban areas, and the government's underestimate of the sheer difficulties of planning, building and organizing the new institutions. In the first few months the government was reluctant to give precise indications of the level of support that had been pledged by industry, but it was evident that it was far lower than anticipated.

By January 1987 no announcement about sponsors had been made, and many of the leading companies had publicly stated that they would not be sponsoring a CTC. As a result, in an attempt to encourage sponsorship, the government announced that it would introduce legislation to safeguard industrial funding against abolition of the scheme by any future Labour government or any collapse of the scheme. This promised legislation was eventually embodied in Section 105 of the 1988 Education Reform Act. The CTCs were initially funded under existing legislation permitting the Secretary of State to give grants to private schools. The main purpose of the new legislation was to protect the investment of sponsors against any change of government. In the original Education Reform Bill of November 1987, Section 80 (as it was then) had just five subsections. The first reiterated the power of the Secretary of State to make payments to CTCs, the second gave the characteristics of such schools (to be in an urban area, provide free education to children aged 11 to 18 of different abilities drawn wholly or mainly from the area in which the school is situated, and have a broad curriculum with an emphasis on science and technology), and the third gave the Secretary of State power to make the grant dependent upon certain conditions to be specified in individual agreements. The fourth and the fifth subsections were the heart of the legislation, for they stated that funding would be given for a period of not less than five years, and that payments could not be terminated with less than five years' notice. Sponsors were also indemnified for expenditure incurred in establishing and maintaining a CTC should any future Secretary of State terminate the agreements. It is an indication of the problems that the government was having in finding sponsors that Section 105 of the 1988 Education Reform Act, as it eventually became, raised the five-year minimum funding and termination limits to seven years and clarified the financial details of what would happen if the school was discontinued or changed its character.

Another development in early 1987 was that Cyril Taylor was appointed adviser to Kenneth Baker to help in the process of establishing CTCs, and was henceforward to play a major part in negotiating for possible sites and encouraging potential sponsors. In May 1987 he was appointed as chairman of the new City Technology Colleges Trust, a charitable organization established 'with the approval of the Secretary of State for Education and Science' to assist the initial twenty CTCs. The Trust has been funded by sponsors and the DES, but it was expected that the DES funding would reduce sharply after the first two years of operation. Under Sir Cyril Taylor's chairmanship, the Trust has actively sought out new sites and sponsors and has acted as a broker to bring together all those involved. Throughout the following months of uncertainty and changes of direction he was constantly to claim that the problem was with sites and Labour councils rather than sponsors, but his reluctance to give the names of these sponsors did little to boost confidence.

The City Technology College, Kingshurst, in Solihull, was the first of the CTCs to be formally designated. The process by which the site was selected is discussed in Chapter 2. Here, in the context of the development of the national plan, it is sufficient to note that both of the major financial backers of the CTC Kingshurst were already major donors to Conservative Party funds (*Labour Research* 1988). The major sponsor, the British wing of the multi-national Hanson plc, gave £102,000 to the Conservative Party in 1987, while the second most important sponsor, Lucas Industries, gave £17,500. Solihull was one of the few Conservative-controlled metropolitan boroughs, and only a few years previously its Leader of the Council and Chair of Education Committee had shown themselves keen to try to reintroduce selective education.

It might have been expected that the announcement in February 1987 of both a site and sponsors in Solihull would have acted to encourage others, but the attack from industrialists actually intensified. In March the Director of the Industrial Society called on the government to admit that the CTC plan was a failure. It had failed, he claimed, because the government had asked industry to contribute far too much money and also because it was asking industry to support an overtly selective system, an act which could ruin existing relationships with state schools and LEAs (Vulliamy 1987). That same month the government was even attacked from within by an internal pressure group calling itself the Conservative Education Association.

Undoubtedly obtaining suitable sites for the CTCs was proving more difficult than expected. Even though many of the local authorities were experiencing falling school rolls and closing schools as a result, the Labour-controlled councils were refusing to release land or disused school buildings. But sponsors were also a problem. By May 1987 only two further major sponsorship gifts had been pledged and both of these were from retail chains rather than manufacturing industries. Dixons electrical had agreed to sponsor a CTC in South Yorkshire but no site was available at the time of announcement, and the Harris/Queensway stores group was prepared to donate £1 million towards a site in Wandsworth. Dixons' generosity was rewarded by the National Association of Schoolmasters/Union of Women Teachers annual conference, which voted overwhelmingly to support a boycott of products of companies supporting CTCs. What slight effect this boycott may have had was probably felt more by the easily recognizable Dixons than the less well known Hanson plc companies.

The uncertainty of the forthcoming general election meant that some companies were reluctant to announce their support before the Conservative Party was returned to government, but the fourth major sponsor was prepared to become part of the pre-election publicity. In early June Mr Harry Djanogly, chairman of the Nottingham Manufacturing Textile Company, pledged £1 million of his own money to help fund a CTC in Nottingham.

After the Conservatives were re-elected in 1987, Kenneth Baker visited some 'magnet' schools in Washington and New York. These schools are usually neighbourhood high schools which have special enrichment programmes to act as a magnet to draw other pupils from a wider area (Metz 1986; Cooper 1987). There is a range of schools with different specialisms; some are for science and mathematics or even aeronautical engineering, while others are for dance or art. Kenneth Baker returned to the UK with a new justification for the CTCs in terms of their 'magnet' status, which echoed earlier arguments put forward by Caroline Cox (1985). However, in the USA magnet schools had been introduced mainly to serve social and egalitarian purposes, in particular, to aid racial desegregation. The earlier involuntary bussing of pupils from one area to another had been deeply resented, especially as it was usually black children who had been bussed to white areas, so special facilities had been put into selected inner-city black schools to tempt white children in. Although still the subject of debate, some of the USA magnet schools have met with considerable success in terms of integration, but the relevance of this to the CTC concept, which had been formulated in part to legitimize inequality of provision, selection and competition, was not easy to see.

By the time the first CTC opened in September 1988, the original idea had been considerably modified.

First, the strict separation of the CTCs from LEA control had been relaxed as it had been announced that LEAs could run their own CTCs if they wished.

Second, negotiations had been started with a number of voluntary controlled schools to encourage them to close and then re-open as CTCs with additional capital funding from DES.

Third, the proportion of the capital expenditure that was to be provided by government to establish the new colleges had risen to about 80 per cent of the total capital expenditure. In the case of Nottingham CTC, which was the first college to be specially designed and built as a CTC on a new site, the government was paying about £7 million from the Treasury. At that point, the total amount of formal DES funding allowed for the CTC programme had risen to some £90 million over the years from 1987/88 to 1990/91, compared with a pledged £25 million of private sponsorship money. Even this £25 million was not as generous as it looked, for it took no account of the tax concessions given to companies making charitable donations.

Fourth, the CTC Trust had admitted to a change in policy such that they were no longer looking to create new schools which might threaten other LEA schools: the new aim was to buy-up schools in use and phase in the CTC through a process of transition. Cyril Taylor also admitted that it was hoped that this revised plan, with guarantees that children actually in the schools would not be turned out, would help to reduce opposition from parents. However, the revised policy was also linked to the fact that the original cost estimates for refurbishing and equipping redundant schools and for building on new sites had been 'woefully underestimated by the DES' (Nash 1988).

Fifth, instead of seeking just one major backer for each CTC, the Trust was now seeking consortia of small local businesses. It had been recognized that there were few single backers willing to donate the large sums required to support a CTC by themselves.

At the point of Solihull's opening in September 1988, there were seven other CTCs at various stages of negotiation. The newly built college at Nottingham and the revamped redundant Roman Catholic school at Middlesbrough were due to open in 1989. Nottingham had already added to controversy by promising a no-strike clause in its terms and conditions for teachers. It has also introduced a five-term year of eight weeks in each term, giving two weeks more work every year. Major funding for the Middlesbrough CTC included donations from John Hall, a property developer, the Davy Corporation, British Steel and BAT Industries, formerly known as British and American Tobacco. BAT's involvement had caused concern amongst the non-smoking and health education lobbies. When it opened, Macmillan College (as it was eventually called) made a further stir by teaching some subjects in Spanish and providing each pupil with a Z88 portable computer. Other plans were more hazy. An agreement had been made to buy

the redundant buildings of another Roman Catholic school in
Gateshead. At Bexley, the Mercers' Company had a plan which
involved the closure of Riverside School and its reopening as a
CTC. At Lewisham there was a long-running battle about Haber-
dashers' Aske's Hatcham Boys' and Girls' schools, which were to
be turned into a CTC. In Dartford, the buildings of the Downs
School, a large comprehensive due for reorganization, were to
form the base for a CTC, while in Croydon, Richard Branson and
British Phonographic Industries were planning a CTC for the
Technology of the Arts in a further redundant school building.
The 1988 Education Reform Act was amended in the late stages
specifically so that this City College for the Technology of the Arts
(CCTA) could take advantage of the CTC legislation. The CTC
plan had already led to a strange mixture of schools and it was to
become even more diverse as time passed.

2

The educational and political context: Solihull and Birmingham

The original booklet from the DES (1986) which described the government's plans for City Technology Colleges included a list of twenty-six possible locations. This included four in the West Midlands: Wolverhampton, Sandwell, Coventry and Birmingham. Birmingham was probably the most important of the four in terms of the credibility of the scheme, for Handsworth, which was included in the Inner City Initiative and still remembered for its ethnic riots of the early 1980s, was explicitly suggested for a site.

However, all four of the West Midlands Metropolitan Boroughs mentioned were Labour controlled, and each quickly made it clear that it would not co-operate with plans for CTCs. Of the seven Boroughs in the West Midlands, Solihull was the most likely to offer the government help. As this chapter will show, the rather strange geographical shape and location of Solihull, its historic development as a Borough, its recent attempts at educational re-organization and the personalities of several of the leading Conservative councillors all acted together to make it especially likely that the CTC concept would be given a good reception.

The maps in Figures 1 and 2 show that the site chosen for The City Technology College, Kingshurst, was in the north of Solihull, only about a quarter of a mile from the border with Birmingham. As is discussed further in Chapter 6, the catchment area has changed slightly since the CTC was first opened, but it includes this northern region of Solihull and a substantial part of adjoining east Birmingham. Within the catchment area are five secondary schools in north Solihull, four secondary schools in east

Birmingham and about thirty-six primary schools evenly divided between the two areas. Thus, although Birmingham local education authority had firmly opposed CTCs, this one in Solihull would draw pupils from within its borders.

Solihull and its educational system

At first sight Solihull appears to be far from the sort of inner-city deprived area which Kenneth Baker had in mind when he launched the CTC initiative. It is predominantly a middle-class affluent area which acts as a 'stockbroker belt' for Birmingham, and has a university entry rate of 12 per cent – about double the national average for all metropolitan boroughs. However, first impressions can be misleading, for the Metropolitan Borough of Solihull is better thought of as three distinct geographical and social areas which were brought together in 1974 for reasons which had more to do with the politics of the West Midlands than with the creation of a logical unit. The southern area consists of the old county borough, which centres on Solihull village, but also includes much of the suburban sprawl between it and Birmingham. This southern area is dominated by the affluent middle-class, living

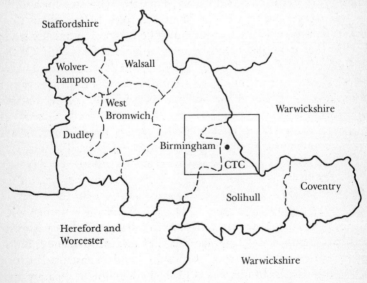

Figure 1

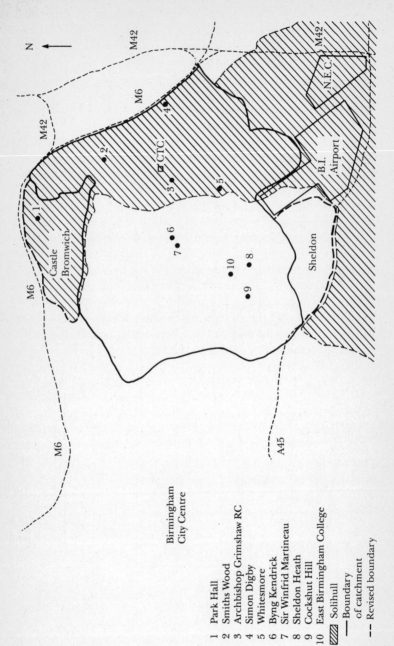

N ←

M42

M42

M6

M6

M6

M42

Castle
Bromwich

1

2

CTC

3

4

5

6

7

10

9

8

Sheldon

B.I.
Airport

N.E.C.

A45

Birmingham
City Centre

1 Park Hall
2 Smiths Wood
3 Archbishop Grimshaw RC
4 Simon Digby
5 Whitesmore
6 Byng Kendrick
7 Sir Winfrid Martineau
8 Sheldon Heath
9 Cockshut Hill
10 East Birmingham College

⧄⧄⧄ Solihull
——— Boundary
        of catchment
– – – Revised boundary

Figure 2

in expensive housing and being well served by a wide variety of shops and entertainments. Here also are the Council offices, the Central Library complex, the Magistrates' Courts and a Conference Centre. To the east of this old county borough stretches the second part of Solihull Metropolitan Borough which is less clearly defined. It covers a largely rural area, and is relatively sparsely populated, with several upper-middle-class commuter villages serving Birmingham and Coventry.

The north of the borough is in sharp contrast to both of these first two areas. Chelmsley Wood consists almost entirely of 1960s Birmingham overspill council estates and is predominantly working class. The Chelmsley Wood Estate was developed by the then Birmingham City Council between 1966 and 1973. It has some 15,000 dwellings and was built as part of the City's slum clearance and rehousing programme (*Official Guide* 1987). Bordering on Chelmsley Wood is Kingshurst, built mainly in the 1950s in response to Birmingham's post-war housing demands. There is some private housing here, but a major part is the Kingshurst Hall Estate, another Birmingham overspill development. This northern part of Solihull is geographically remote from the south, with Birmingham International Airport, the National Exhibition Centre and the main Coventry Road (A45) acting as a divide between the two parts. Two-thirds of Solihull's council-built housing is in this northern area, and it was managed by Birmingham until 1980 (Biddle 1985). Since Solihull took over management, Kingshurst has been targeted for improvement, with some unpopular maisonettes being demolished or refurbished, and the complete renovation of some of the high-rise accommodation. Further north again is the Park Hall Estate and Castle Bromwich, which has a higher proportion of both older and new middle-class housing. In summary, while the whole of this northern area of Solihull has some pockets of high-quality middle-class housing, the bulk is still relatively poor, with patches of extremely poor accommodation. The CTC is sited roughly in the centre of this northern area.

An indication of the social class composition of the catchment area of the CTC can be derived from the 1981 Census. Small area statistics on wards are available in published form and, while the wards do not neatly coincide with the CTC catchment area, there is sufficient broad agreement to make comparisons worthwhile. There will also have been changes to the social class composition of the area since 1981, but these are unlikely to have dramatically altered the broad picture. Table 2.1 gives the social class of heads of households in 1981 for the five north Solihull wards according to occupation using the Registrar General's Classification. Under the classification social class I covers professional and similar occupations, II represents intermediate occupations, III is divided into non-manual skilled occupations (N) and manual skilled occupations (M), IV is partly skilled occupations and V is unskilled occupations. Those heads of household who are retired or in the armed forces are classified separately.

The distribution of social class can be seen to be very similar for four of the five wards, with a striking skew towards the working class. There were relatively few heads of households of social class I, II or IIIN. Castle Bromwich stands in contrast to the other four wards with a high proportion of social class II and significantly larger proportions of social class I, II and IIIN. Castle Bromwich had a social class composition more middle class than the national average. In 1981 91.7 per cent of household heads within these five north Solihull wards were born in the UK, 4.3 per cent were of Irish origin and 3.2 per cent from the New Commonwealth or Pakistan. As the majority of housing was on post-war estates, all five wards had an age distribution which was younger than the national average.

Solihull Metropolitan Borough has always had a Conservative majority on the local Council. In 1989, for example, there were twenty-nine Conservative, fourteen Labour and eight mixed others. The Labour-held wards were predominantly in the north, where they held all of the wards except Castle Bromwich ('a Tory finger') at the extreme north. Many of the Conservative and Labour councillors have served in that capacity for many years.

Table 2.1   Social class of heads of households for five north Solihull wards 1981

	I	II	IIIN	IIIM	IV	V	Forces	Retired
Castle Bromwich	3.6	22.7	13.9	28.1	9.0	1.1	2.5	19.1
Chelmsley Wood	0.2	6.9	6.9	32.3	19.2	5.1	3.6	25.8
Fordbridge	0.8	5.8	4.2	33.2	21.1	6.1	2.8	26.0
Kingshurst	1.2	8.1	6.3	29.1	17.1	5.1	8.1	25.0
Smithswood	0.7	7.3	7.8	32.9	18.0	5.5	4.0	23.8
English average	3.9	16.8	9.2	21.2	10.6	3.4	2.0	32.8

Source: Census 10 per cent sample

There is a mixed pattern of educational provision within Solihull which reflects the origins of the borough in the 1974 local authority reorganization. In the north of the borough there were originally six secondary schools inherited from Warwickshire. All of these were already comprehensive, three (Archbishop Grimshaw RC, Park Hall and Whitesmore) having some sixth form provision, and the other three (Smiths Wood, Simon Digby and Kingshurst) being for 11 – 16 only. In addition a small secondary school (Culey Green) had been temporarily established in buildings belonging to Birmingham to deal with a short-term increase in numbers in the area. In the old county borough in the south, the five grammar schools and eight high schools (with the addition of one new school) had been reorganized in 1974 into ten 11–16 comprehensive schools, with a purpose-built sixth form college established at the same time to cater for post-16 academic education. In the east the only school (Heart of England), formerly a grammar school, became an 11–18 comprehensive school in 1974. In addition to the schools provision there is also a college of technology, located in the south. Although theoretically it serves all of the borough, only a small proportion of students come from the north.

In the early 1980s falling school rolls had led to the closure of a number of schools. In the north, Culey Green and Kingshurst ceased to admit pupils in September 1984 and finally closed in July 1988; two schools were similarly closed in the south. The Culey Green decision was straightforward, as this was the school which had been established in a building on a temporary lease and was actually within Birmingham. The decision to close Kingshurst was made mainly on the basis of low pupil numbers in relation to permanent places available in the building, its geographical position in relation to other schools and the fact that it was housed in inferior quality buildings compared with neighbouring secondary schools.

It is worth noting that at the time the decision to close Kingshurst was made, one of the two options discussed by the Education Committee was to use part of the premises for a tertiary college. There had been long-standing concern amongst both Labour and Conservative councillors that the staying-on rates in the north of the borough were substantially lower than in the south. It was widely felt that some non-school post-16 provision in the north would encourage more pupils to continue with their full-time education, and an unofficial bipartisan policy had developed that this would be done when one of the schools in the area closed. In the event, the extra expenditure that would be necessary and claims that the plan was unviable led the Conservative majority to change its mind. It was decided that the Kingshurst buildings and site should be put up for sale once the school had finally closed.

Staying-on rates within the north of the borough are undoubtedly low. In 1988 about 18 per cent stayed at school after 16 in the three schools with sixth form provision. Most of these studied one-year courses. The proportion staying on has nearly doubled in ten years, but the structure of post-16 provision within the north makes these figures misleading, for they do not include further education or provision outside the borough. In 1987, for example, some 25.7 per cent of north Solihull pupils transferred to all forms of full-time post-16 education. In practice Whitesmore now provides sixth form education only for a few one-year students: sixth form provision is concentrated in the other two schools. The presence of a sixth form within the school dramatically affects staying-on rates. In 1988/89 Archbishop Grimshaw achieved a rate of 56 per cent staying on past 16, while Park Hall had 37 per cent. In both cases, fewer than half of these students were entered for one-year courses rather than two.

Birmingham and its education system

The social class composition of the east Birmingham part of the CTC catchment area is indicated by the figures in Table 2.2. Again, these figures relate to 1981 and, while ward boundaries do not correspond exactly to the catchment area boundary, they are close enough to be meaningful.

Table 2.2   Social class of heads of households for four east Birmingham wards 1981

	I	II	IIIN	IIIM	IV	V	Forces	Retired
Shard End	0.7	4.8	11.0	17.7	15.6	6.1	3.7	40.4
Hodge Hill	0.9	7.3	12.6	17.3	14.1	4.3	3.6	40.0
Yardley	1.1	8.4	13.6	17.6	14.0	4.4	4.0	36.9
Sheldon	1.2	7.6	16.0	20.0	13.3	3.0	1.7	37.2
English average	3.9	16.9	9.2	21.2	10.6	3.4	2.0	32.8

Source: Census 10 per cent sample

It can be seen that the area was predominantly working class, with only small numbers of social class I and II households. In 1981 there were also significantly more retired people in this east Birmingham part of the CTC catchment area than in the north Solihull part, a feature which may well have changed markedly since that date.

Birmingham is the largest education authority in the country now that the Inner London Education Authority (ILEA) has been abolished. In 1989 it catered for 168,000 pupils, employing 55,700 teachers in nearly 500 schools. At the secondary level, Birmingham had forty-two 11–16 comprehensive schools, twenty-nine 11–18 or 12–18 comprehensive schools, eight grammar schools and four sixth form colleges. There were also eight further education colleges with 39,000 students and 1,300 lectures. Birmingham Metropolitan Borough is Labour controlled, but power has alternated with the Conservatives up to 1984, which has led to the retention of a highly selective grammar school system. In the north of Birmingham, in Sutton Coldfield, which was part of Warwickshire until 1974, one boys' grammar school and one girls' grammar school take about 150 new pupils each year at age 12. Parents have to apply for their child to take an optional test in the November preceding proposed entry, which is taken at the grammar schools, but administered by Birmingham Education Department. Selection is based on the result of this written paper and an assessment by the child's primary school Headteacher.

The bulk of Birmingham is served by six more grammar schools, which accept a total of about 600 pupils at age 11. Five of these schools are part of the King Edward VI Foundation (which also includes the two private King Edward's schools) and there is also the Handsworth Grammar School for boys. Four of these schools are for boys and two for girls. In February 1989 the Law Lords ruled that Birmingham was acting unlawfully by providing 540 places at its total of five boys' grammar schools and 360 places at its three girls' grammar schools. The nature of the Foundation schools mean that they are difficult for the LEA to change, but one plan was to change Handsworth Grammar school to co-education. In November 1989 the governors refused to do so, and Birmingham has yet to comply with the law on equal opportunities. Again, parents have to apply for their child to take a test, and places are allocated on the basis of these results and the Headteachers' reports. It is highly competitive, with about 5,000 children (about half of those eligible) taking the test for transfer at 11, for just over 600 places. About 9 per cent of the age range is selected each year. Preference is given to those residing within Birmingham, so it is pointless for those outside Birmingham to apply. It is worth noting that the Birmingham selection procedure for grammar schools, in part, selects on the basis of ability and willingness to pay as well as academic ability as 'Pupils attending selective schools do not receive free transport from the Education Authority if an appropriate course exists in an all-ability school within three miles of the home' (Birmingham City Council 1990).

Within the catchment area of the CTC in east Birmingham there were once seven secondary schools. Falling school rolls have led to the closure of Alderlea in the mid-1980s, and Longmeadow and Archbishop Williams RC secondary schools in 1988. The four remaining schools are Sir Wilfrid Martineau, Byng Kendrick Central, Cockshut Hill and Sheldon Heath. All four schools are 11 to 18, Byng Kendrick Central and Sir Wilfrid Martineau sharing a site and a Sixth Form.

It is finally worth noting that there are no private secondary schools within the catchment area of the CTC. The West Midlands as a whole has about seventeen 'respectable' private secondary schools, but some of these are for children up to the age of 16 only, and others are simply too far away from the CTC to be considered. One of the few which could be slightly affected by the CTC is Solihull School, which is in Solihull town centre and takes secondary boys from 11 to 18 and girls from 16 to 18. Somewhat nearer to Kingshurst, in Sutton Coldfield, is Highclare School Ltd, which takes secondary girls from 11 to 19. In Birmingham itself the nearest 11 to 18 private schools are the King Edward's School for boys and the King Edward VI School for Girls, both in Edgbaston, south of the city. In practice, the presence of the CTC has had minimal effect on any of these private schools.

TVEI and the technological curriculum

Although north Solihull and the adjacent area of east Birmingham have a social class composition close to that which might be seen as appropriate for a CTC, technological education and training was well advanced in both areas before the CTC was proposed. Solihull joined the Technical and Vocational Education Initiative in

1984, with a plan which involved a consortium of seven secondary schools, including three of the five in the CTC catchment area. The first two years of the four-year 14–18 course were entirely school-based, while the second two years involved the schools with sixth forms, Solihull College of Technology and Solihull Sixth Form College. Broad specialist subject areas were developed in five of the schools – food technology, manufacturing technology, caring services, commerce and business studies, and media technology – and appropriate facilities provided. Simon Digby developed media technology, while Park Hall specialized in manufacturing technology. TVEI was funded for five years until 1989, and the funding brought extra teachers and equipment to all of the participating schools. As the first two years of the course were entirely school based, the three north Solihull schools involved were able to buy considerable CDT and information technology equipment. Those staff already within the schools who became involved with TVEI also benefited from learning and experimenting with new skills and teaching styles. The Solihull scheme was arranged such that a proportion of students specifically opted for the course, and were bussed between schools to take courses in their subject area specialisms. Pupils from various schools were taught in the same classes, and it was widely reported by staff in the three participating north Solihull schools, that the presence of more middle-class pupils from the south of the borough had a good social and work influence on their own pupils. Several of the Heads indicated that they thought that the mixing helped to dispel some of the myths held by both parents and pupils in each part of the borough about each other. As one Head put it: 'It didn't do any harm to have a few Volvo's in the car park on parents' night for a change'. In 1989 TVE Extension provided less funding; bussing of pupils has from that time been only between the north schools. The schools in the south now have their own separate system, and this improvement in social mixing has ceased.

In view of the decision to introduce a CTC into the north Solihull area, it is worth looking at one of these three TVEI schools in some detail: Park Hall School. Park Hall School is the most popular school in the area, but this account of one school does not mean that similar activities were not occurring in other schools in the catchment area. Although sometimes less well developed, all of the north Solihull schools were involved in various industrial links, work experience schemes and vocational courses. Park Hall School in the very north of the borough in Castle Bromwich has about 1,200 11–16 pupils and a sixth form of about 130. As explained later in Chapter 6, there were some changes to the catchment area of the CTC after the first year of operation, and originally Park Hall School had not been included within the area, although one of its three main feeder primary schools had been. From the second year onwards all three feeder primary schools and Park Hall itself have been included within the CTC catchment area. The school has a dynamic Head, Sidney Slater (1987; 1988a; 1988b), who has published articles on curriculum innovation, education and industry, and appraisal. He started building links with industrialists in 1971 while Head of Department in a school in London. As the Head of Abraham Moss High School, Manchester, he had worked with groups of industrialists to develop courses for lower-attaining pupils, and had obtained additional DES funding to support the venture. On appointment to Park Hall School in early 1984, Slater fought to have his school included in TVEI and quickly established a steering group, which included industrialists from three major local companies – Land Rover Ltd, Lucas Aerospace and Cincinatti – to develop the first two years of the TVEI Manufacturing Technology course. This programme for the 14–16 age group was taught on two mornings a week and covered applied physics, technology, and microelectronics and computing. It included work-experience and a residential element. The success of this steering group led to a far closer partnership between Park Hall and Land Rover in the development of post-16 provision (Slater and Hanley 1989). A new course in manufacturing science and technology was gradually developed by a team of seventeen teachers and industrialists from Land Rover. Pairs of teachers and industrialists worked together to develop a curriculum in the seven topic areas of the course – management, finance, materials, computer-aided engineering, workshop practice, modern languages in industry, and data management. Most of the work was done by teachers and industrialists on a voluntary basis in free time in evenings and weekends; two residential weekends were held where course outlines were developed and relationships established. The whole of the modular course was designed and written in a full collaboration between teachers and industrialists and, almost uniquely, the group applied for and received a special school contract from the Manpower Services Commission to help with the costs.

The closeness of the collaboration was attested by various

teachers and by Land Rover industrialists, who were involved with
the course. One key element was that most of the Land Rover
personnel were at manager or director level. They were directly
involved with day-to-day practice yet prepared to give some of
their free time to be involved with shaping and developing what
they regarded as a very worthwhile venture. One of these managers explained

> Well, one of the very significant things that happened was
> that we got some of the examination papers that these TVEI
> people were going to work at, and I brought them back here
> [to Land Rover] and I asked some of our brightest graduates
> what it meant to them. It was all about space rockets and
> similar things – nothing that related to anything they had
> done since they came here. We took a broad cross-section of
> people and we decided that the curriculum didn't really
> match with what went on here. When I say 'here', I mean in
> industry, and not necessarily just Land Rover. So we asked
> ourselves, what does go on? I asked people, what is it that you
> actually do? What are the skills that you think manufacturing
> technology is about?

The final course in management science and technology is a two-
year all-ability programme, which takes one day each week and is
combined with other academic studies. It also includes work experience, work shadowing and a residential period. It is unusual
not just in the way it was developed, but because Land Rover still
play a significant part in evaluating, assessing, up-dating and even
teaching parts of it. The staff in the school are aware that the course
has limitations, for example, the lack of input from unions and the
limited number of teachers involved, but plan to rectify these
difficulties in the future.

Originally the idea was just to give a Land Rover/Park Hall
certificate for the course, but the success of the scheme led to the
idea of seeking external validation. The steering group had been
approached by an A level Board, but wished to ensure that the
course was validated for all abilities, which was eventually achieved
through Birmingham Polytechnic, which gives it A level
equivalence for a pass with distinction or merit. About twenty-five
students per year now take the course. There is a certain irony to
the fact that the status of the course was endorsed by Kenneth
Baker who presented the certificate to one of the successful students

at the British Association for Advancement of Science Exhibition in 1988.

Although this particular course has gained much publicity, the Head emphasizes that the school is not just a science and technology school. He sees science, technology and industrial links as the school's marketing niche, but the school runs and encourages a full range of academic, cultural, social and sporting activities as well. There are numerous visits, sports fixtures, music and dramatic productions. At A level it offers nineteen A level subjects, including two modern languages, art, music and sociology, however not all of these subjects obtain sufficient takers to run each year.

Park Hall has several other aspects of its curriculum worthy of mention. In September 1988 a two-subject entry modular GCSE in business structures and technology was introduced; it had been developed jointly with Smiths Wood and Simon Digby Schools, and industrialists representing ten different industries. The school runs an information technology (IT) course from the first year, and includes IT in as much of its teaching as resources allow. Short teacher secondments are arranged between the school and various companies, and industrialists spend time at the school. Much more unusually, and of particular relevance given the CTCs decision to offer Business and Technicians Education Council awards, the Park Hall also runs a BTEC National Diploma in Business and Finance, which the school offers because it wishes to break away from the narrowness of A level. BTEC does not provide a syllabus, so every course has to be developed by individual centres, which are usually further education colleges. In 1988/89 there were ninety-five students taking A levels only or A levels plus BTEC. They gained an average of 2.0 pass grades at A level. At GCSE level 264 fifth form pupils gained 642 passes grades A to C, an average of 2.4 per pupil. While neither of these averages is high, they have increased over the last few years and must be considered in the context of the intake. Park Hall was one of the first schools to become a BTEC centre on its own, and was given this right in part because of its close school–industry links. The course started in 1987, and had been developed before the CTC idea had even been announced. Since 1990 the school has offered a wider range of BTEC courses, some in conjunction with Archbishop Grimshaw RC and the College of Technology.

Whether this degree of collaboration between industrialists and a school is desirable or not is something on which educationists would differ. However, such strong links are clearly what the government sees as desirable, and what it has tried to encourage through TVEI and CTCs. What is important to note here is that Park Hall and other local schools were involved in this type of activity well before there was any thought of a CTC in the area, and that it was working in collaboration with other LEA schools in developing new curricular and teaching methods.

Similar, although perhaps not so far-reaching, technological developments were occurring in Birmingham, fostered by their TVEI scheme which started in 1983. At that point the Conservatives controlled Birmingham Council, but the TVEI application was agreed by both major parties. The TVEI proposal listed 62 of its 108 secondary schools as having active links with industry. This included Byng Kendrick Central School with a Young Enterprise Scheme, but not Sir Wilfrid Martineau which was on the same site, but at that time had a Head who was reported to be antagonistic to computers and information technology. However, these two schools, together with the East Birmingham Technical College, formed one of the six partnerships involved in Birmingham's TVEI scheme. This meant an extra four or five specialist teachers per school and significant extra funding for the five-year duration of TVEI. The schools and the college devised a 14–18 curriculum which was co-ordinated through timetable alignments between the three sites, and involved BTEC and CPVE (Certificate of Pre-Vocational Education) certification. The TVEI curriculum for 1986–88 involved all students having four periods of IT per week and a sixteen-period modular curriculum including science, CDT, business studies, food studies and textiles, in addition to normal courses in English and mathematics. All students were profiled, took part in nine industrial visits, had an industrial tutor, undertook a one-week residential course and took part in a three-week work experience.

As with north Solihull, the experience of TVEI in Birmingham seems to have been generally very positive. It gave a chance to broaden and develop curricula, to enhance links with industry and, perhaps most important, brought extra resources, equipment and staff. Implementation was not without difficulties, but the way in which the technical and vocational aspects were fairly broadly defined largely dispelled earlier fears from teachers that TVEI would lead to a narrow vocationalism. The far less generous funding of the TVE Extension programme was seen as a major limitation to what the schools would be able to do in the future.

Solihull's attempt to reintroduce selective education

In the context of being prepared to offer a site for the CTC and the accusation by many of the CTC opponents that this was an attempt to introduce grammar-school-type selection by the back door, it is of interest to consider an earlier attempt to reintroduce selective education in Solihull (Walford and Jones 1986). In early September 1983 the Director of Education for Solihull was asked by the Council Policy Committee to prepare a feasibility report on the possibility of reintroducing selective schools into the borough. The ten-page report was presented to the Education Committee and the Policy Committee on Secondary Education in late September (Humphrey 1983) and suggested that one or two of the most obviously academically successful comprehensive schools should be transformed into selective 11–16 schools which would then serve the top 10–15 per cent of the ability range. Selection was to be on the basis of a combination of longitudinal assessments and 'objective' testing.

The plan came about as a result of changes to school catchment areas, caused by the closure of two schools in the south that were announced in July 1983. Whether by accident or design, the main changes were to the catchment areas of Tudor Grange, the highly prestigious ex-grammar school in Solihull village. Parents who had carefully bought expensive houses within the previous catchment area objected strongly, and it was evident that some further changes would have to be made to placate traditional Conservative voters. The plan for a selective system was in part a response to this parental pressure, but was also justified by the belief that academically able children were not being adequately catered for in some of the schools – especially some in the north. The proportion of pupils gaining five or more O level passes or equivalent in 1982 was given in this report to be 36.8 per cent in the south but only 13.1 per cent in the north (including Heart of England, actually in the east).

What seems to have occurred is that the Leader of the Council (Robert Meacham) and the Chairman of the Education

Committee (Michael Ellis) were keen to bring back selection and, without prior consultation with committee members, recommended that a feasibility report be prepared for the Education Committee. It is worth noting that those involved had private discussions about selection with Stuart Sexton, at that time adviser to Sir Keith Joseph (Bowcott 1983), and Bob Dunn, then Under-Secretary of State for Education, in advance of presenting their plans.

Somewhat to the surprise of the proponents, the first indication that selective education was being reconsidered provoked a massive public outcry. The local and national press took up the story and concerted opposition developed. While they might have anticipated some protest from teachers' unions and opposition party supporters, this was supplemented by action from parents and pupils. A protest group was formed, letters were sent to councillors, MPs and the media, demonstrations outside the Council Chamber were organized and independent public meetings were held. In the face of such opposition the Council meeting at which the report was presented on 21 September was stormy. While Robert Meacham reaffirmed his wish to see selective schools, more than 100 parents demonstrated outside and more packed the public gallery. The Council voted in favour of selection 'in principle' only and asked for a more detailed report. This second report (Humphrey 1984) was published in February 1984 and suggested that only one school should become selective. The momentum of the protest campaign had been maintained throughout the winter months, and by February it was evident that there was substantial opposition to the proposals from a very large proportion of the voting public, including many who had paid heavily for the privilege of buying a house near to recognized 'good' schools for their children. They had no wish to risk their investment by subjecting their children to tests which they might fail. Their continued pressure led to the complete and embarrassing abandonment of the idea. Several of the names associated with this proposal for selection recur in the decision to welcome a CTC into Solihull.

Local financial management of schools in Solihull

Another important feature of Solihull's educational landscape is the role that it has had in developing local financial management of schools. Robert Meacham again was a major influence. Two years before his election to Leader of the Council in May 1983, Meacham had been thrust into the position of Chairman of the Education Committee at Solihull with no previous service on the Education Committee. The result was the first major experiment with local management of schools – or financial autonomy of schools, as it is known in Solihull. This particular educational development eventually met with considerable success and was seen as beneficial by most Headteachers in the borough. It also received considerable attention in the academic press (for example Humphrey and Thomas 1986; Thomas *et al.* 1989) and, along with Cambridge LEA, was the only long-standing example of local financial management which could be used to bolster the plans for delegation of financial management to schools contained within the 1988 Education Reform Act (Walford 1990a: 98).

In the light of its importance nationally, and for what it reveals about the complexion of Solihull Council, it is worth noting how these changes originally came about in Solihull. Luckily we have a publicly available account from the Director of Education at the time, Colin Humphrey (1988), who later wrote bluntly about how he had seen the changes in a booklet published by the Institute for Economic Affairs:

> Cllr Robert K. Meacham . . . gave an address in his constituency on how to reduce educational spending by £1 million. His electors told him in no uncertain terms that they did not wish to reduce the cost of education but would rather pay more to provide a better service for their children. Undeterred and re-elected he raised his sights to a saving of £5 million. . . . Standard of service was about to become second fiddle to cost effectiveness.
>
> The role of Councillor Meacham was crucial to the introduction of financial autonomy in Solihull. He held the view that if you applied the same sort of procedures to running a school as he used in running a small business, and ignore the fact that one is there to provide a service and the other to make a profit, there must then be some improvement in performance, since if you are spending your own money you will exercise more care than if you are spending someone else's.
>
> (Humphrey 1988: 1)

Humphrey makes it clear that Meacham's prime aim was undoubtedly to save money, rather than the more efficient use of existing resources. The original small-scale scheme was introduced half way through the financial year 1981/82 and involved a 2 per cent reduction in planned funding for the one secondary school and the sixth form college involved. As the scheme expanded this deduction was reduced in size and was finally removed by 1985, when the scheme was put on a 'value for money' basis. However, Humphrey warns those in schools who have responsibility for finance that 'Reserves should be kept to a minimum safe level and other unspent funds clearly marked for projects – otherwise hard pressed Councils might see reserves as justification for education cuts' (Humphrey 1988: 12).

The sale of the Kingshurst site

The last year of pupils at Kingshurst Secondary School were due to leave in July 1988. For some years before this, the Council Land Subcommittee had been trying to find a buyer for the school and site. The Land Subcommittee was small and consisted of only Conservative councillors. It reported to the Council Policy Committee, which again consisted only of Conservative members and had the Leader of the Council as its chairman. The task of selling the school was not an easy one, for the buildings were known to be in poor condition – this was one of the reasons why it had been chosen for closure in the first place. Another problem was that it was sited in a green belt, with its land adjoining that of another school and a park, making it very difficult to have obtained permission for change of use for the site. At one point the police tentatively looked at the buildings with a view of converting them into a training college, but there had been no serious enquiries.

Given the character of the Leader of the Council illustrated in the attempts to reintroduce selective education and to save money through financial delegation, it is not surprising that discussions occurred between him, a small number of other key Conservative councillors and the DES soon after the City Technology Colleges were proposed. Bob Dunn, Under-Secretary of State for Education, visited the site in mid-December 1986, and it became known the next week that Solihull were likely to sell the school for a CTC on a long lease. The actual decision 'in principle' to sell the site was made by the Land Subcommittee and the Policy Committee, and not by the Education Committee. The first some of the members of the Education Committee heard of the idea was through an article in the *Sunday Telegraph* – the same newspaper that had been first to carry the news to them some years earlier about proposals to reintroduce selective schools. The Education Committee was asked to look at the implications of the plan only after this 'in principle' decision had been made, and when it did, enough of the members saw advantages for it to go through. The educational advantages were voiced in terms of the extension of parental choice and the provision of good educational facilities without the Council having to pay for them. It was also argued that the CTC might increase competition between the schools in the area and encourage a raising of standards,. The Conservatives did not explicitly justify the CTC in terms of its selectivity of pupils, but it is' hard to believe that this was not also in the minds of some of the proponents. There was no official consultation at all with parents or teachers.

Hanson plc acquired a 125-year lease on the school on behalf of the CTC in February, the official announcement being made on 24 February 1987 by Kenneth Baker and representatives of Hanson Trust and Lucas Industries. Hanson plc paid £1 million for the lease, and was given an eighteen-month option to pull out in case Labour won the forthcoming general election. At that point Lucas had not decided to give any financial support, but was going to second a senior manager for four days a week to help with the planning for the new college. There were no other firm financial backers at that time.

Local opposition to the CTC

The announcement and launch of the CTC on 24 February was made in the school hall of the old Kingshurst Secondary School while its remaining pupils were on half-term holiday. Outside the school gates a small group of parents, teachers and predominantly Labour Party supporters protested against the first CTC, arguing that it was unnecessary, an implied insult to local maintained schools, and that the competition was liable to make staff recruitment to those schools increasingly difficult. This demonstration was part of a broad spectrum of opposition which included the local Solihull

Branch of the National Union of Teachers and representatives from the Birmingham Trades Council. These opponents also accused the Council of bringing in a form of selection by the back door, after failing to do so openly a few years before. This was strongly denied by Robert Meacham, but it was widely believed that selection would inevitably cream off the 'best' children from nearby schools. For parents and teachers in the local schools, however, the main concern was that they saw the CTC as making it likely that one of the existing schools would be forced to close. The Conservative councillors had argued that the CTC would bring increased competition to the schools in the north of the borough. The schools were concerned that competition has both winners and losers and they felt the dice to be unfairly loaded against them.

There was certainly good reason for concern. Kingshurst Secondary School had been closed because of falling secondary school rolls in the area, and numbers were predicted to fall still further. The CTC would inevitably be popular as the facilities were planned to be better than those available elsewhere. This might mean that numbers could decline in other schools to such an extent that the Council would be forced to close another in addition to Kingshurst. Meacham argued that the effect on individual schools would be lessened by the fact that the CTC was to have a wide catchment area, and that it would extend well into Birmingham. Fears were not assuaged by such arguments, for logically if the school were to have about 1,000 pupils, and half of this number came from Solihull, it would mean a major reduction in numbers for the other schools. At this stage fears were exacerbated by the expectation that in the first years of opening the CTC would take pupils of all ages from 11 to 15, with a sixth form coming a little later. If this had occurred it would have been very difficult for the schools to have dealt with the effect of the change.

Table 2.3 (see p. 40) shows the situation that the borough faced in 1981 when it decided to close Kingshurst. The 1981 figures are actual numbers of children on roll at each school, and the figures for the remaining years are estimates. The decision to close Culey Green had already been made at this time and the estimates adjusted accordingly.

The accommodation figures in the final column of the table were calculated by the Director of Education applying DES-approved design size. Of the 9,125 places 450 were actually in temporary buildings, including 175 (the greatest number) at

Table 2.3   Real and estimated school rolls in October 1981–6

	1981	1982	1983	1984	1985	1986	Accommodation
Park Hall	1,481	1,528	1,553	1,545	1,502	1,402	1,650
Smith's Wood	1,411	1,420	1,461	1,411	1,363	1,243	1,600
Kingshurst	1,186	1,205	1,216	1,244	1,214	1,170	1,500
Archbishop Grimshaw RC	1,164	1,264	1,219	1,127	1,040	896	1,200
Simon Digby	1,090	1,079	1,104	1,149	1,137	1,077	1,200
Whitesmore	1,233	1,176	1,147	1,097	1,095	1,066	1,475
Culey Green	303	405	499	488	385	280	500
Totals	7,868	8,077	8,199	8,061	7,736	7,134	9,125

Data from Solihull Education Committee papers 26 October 1981

Kingshurst. What is immediately clear is that with 8,675 permanent places and 7,134 pupils predicted for 1986, the original closure of Kingshurst was a very reasonable decision. What was worrying critics of the CTC was that another 500 or so pupils taken out of the local education authority system might lead to yet another school being closed.

A further objection that parents and teachers had to the CTC was that they saw the possibility of it affecting the second stage of the Technical and Vocational Education Initiative within Solihull and Birmingham. It has been shown earlier that both schemes had undoubtedly been successful, and there was concern that the presence of the CTC might affect the forthcoming second stage of TVEI. In particular, there was fear that particularly suitable pupils might be lost to the CTC, that local work experience placements might become overstretched by the new demands and that local teachers in technological and shortage subjects might be more attracted to working in the CTC than in the LEA-maintained schools. Consideration is given to some of these concerns in the next chapters, which describe the nature of Kingshurst CTC as it was in the autumn term of 1989. Discussion of the major issue of selection is delayed until Chapter 6, and the effects that the CTC was actually found to have on local schools is debated in Chapter 7.

3

The college and its staff

The major appointments

Although the announcement of a CTC in Solihull was made in
February 1987, it was September when the Principal was appointed, and not until January 1988 that she formally took office.
As this was the first CTC there were no clear guidelines as to how
to proceed with appointments, but the multi-stage selection procedure adopted involved interviews with representatives of the
major financial sponsors, Her Majesty's Inspectorate and academic
advisers. The advertisements for Principal attracted some 150
applications, including Heads of private and maintained schools,
and people from industry and further and higher education.

The person chosen, Mrs Valerie Bragg, had taught in comprehensive schools, a grammar school and, for one year, at an
independent school. She had been educated in state-maintained
schools, was a graduate from Leicester University and had originally taught zoology, biology and chemistry. She progressed to
Head of Biology, Head of Sixth Form, and Deputy Head at different schools, then became Head of a comprehensive at
Stourport-on-Severn, Herefordshire and Worcestershire. During
her time as Head she had been actively involved in links with
industry and had managed to gain considerable additional funding
from industry and charitable foundations. She had been particularly
concerned to raise parents' expectations for their children, and the
school had increased its Oxbridge entry numbers during her time
there. The school also had a special unit for dyslexic children and a

wide range of scientific and technical initiatives supported by industry. One of the reasons why she had applied for the post was because others talking about the advertisement had spoken as if the job had to go to a man. In choosing Mrs Bragg as first Principal the selectors not only were making a statement about women and technology, but also were appointing a strong and determined pioneer who was to show herself well able to create a new college from scratch with no model to emulate. The nature, organizational structure, ethos and even architecture and internal decoration of Kingshurst CTC are personal statements of the Principal's educational priorities. She has taken advantage of her own position as the first Principal of the first CTC to shape the college as close to her own ideas as possible.

A small group of people representing sponsors and the DES had been working on plans for the CTC since the February 1987 announcement, but at first little could be done physically as the buildings were still being occupied by the last year of pupils of the Kingshurst Secondary School until July 1987. On appointment, Valerie Bragg quickly took charge of the plans for refurbishing the buildings and redesigned the internal layout of classrooms and study areas to suit her own vision for the college. She wanted the college to have the appearance of a modern but friendly suite of offices rather than a school, and for rooms and equipment to be easily accessible for students to use. Rooms were not to be uniform in design, but to have distinctive decoration, furniture and equipment which would be a pleasure to use.

Valerie Bragg also strongly valued cross-curriculum work. In particular, she believed that technology had to be used by everyone and not restricted to particular subject areas, and that the best way to ensure that cross-curriculum work occurred was to inhibit the growth of departments. Thus Kingshurst CTC has no faculties or departments, but has broad and changing areas headed by Area Managers. Wide areas of the curriculum are brought together and this same structure is used for both academic and pastoral organization. There is no separate pastoral structure to divide the staff.

But what is the college like? Here is the first of several cameos.

Monday 2 October 1989, 10.28 am

I'm in the hall, waiting for one of the Principal's weekly assemblies. I'm sitting towards the back, to one side, on one of the single chairs spaced down each side of the hall on which teachers usually sit. One of the Area Managers is at the front of the hall reminding students of 'the rules' as they come in: 'You know you are supposed to be quiet', 'I said no talking', 'Turn round, Kevin', and so on. Another teacher controls the entry of children into the hall through the main doors at the back. There is piano music from one of the music teachers.

The room itself is bright and airy. The old Kingshurst Secondary School hall has been refurbished and redecorated. Everything looks clean and colourful. The ceiling has been lowered and recessed lighting installed; along the walls are upwardly directed decorative side-lights; new grey checked curtains hang in front of the full-length windows on the right, through which can be seen yellow-hatted building workers constructing the next stage of the building. On the wall to the side of the proscenium arch of the stage is a plaque commemorating the official opening of the college by Kenneth Baker in November 1988.

The hall gradually fills with students, who sit on grey and burgundy comfortably padded stacking chairs arranged in two blocks with a central aisle. It is a sea of grey trousers or skirts, burgundy pullovers, white shirts and red and white diagonally striped ties. The simple and relatively cheap uniform is worn by all of the students with only slight modification to emphasize individuality. Some boys seem to be able to get away with white socks rather than the regulation grey, and a few have dark trainers instead of black shoes. Once all the students are quiet, the Area Manager asks them to stand while the Principal, who has been waiting at the back for the last few minutes, walks down the central aisle and takes her place at the podium.

Her talk is on 'quality': quality in work and quality in living. Why was it that medieval stone-masons carved the angels in the far recesses of cathedral roofs as well as those on full view nearer the ground? Mrs Bragg develops her theme by showing eight different posters emphasizing quality. These are too small to be seen from the back, but the students are told that they will have a chance to see them later as they are to be hung around the college. She then praises the students on their behaviour by telling them about a comment a visitor had made about their obvious keenness and enthusiasm.

After the talk Mrs Bragg gives out certificates documenting the award of 10, 50 or 100 merit marks. Students are called to the front in groups of three or four, accompanied by disciplined applause. The honours done, a quick 'Please bow your heads', a prayer, and the Principal leaves. The Area Manager takes control, gives some notices on sports arrangements, and allows the students to leave the hall from the back, one named class at a time. Quiet is maintained until all have left.

The next four chapters will describe some of the major features of the City Technology College, Kingshurst. This chapter is concerned mainly with the college's staff and how teaching is organized. Chapter 4 concentrates on equipment, facilities and the curriculum, Chapter 5 describes the children's reactions to the CTC and Chapter 6 examines the process of selection. All four chapters are based upon a period of data collection and observation conducted within Kingshurst CTC during the autumn term of 1989. During that time I observed classroom teaching, meetings of staff and daily morning briefings, discussed the college with staff and students and attended several after-school activities. There were numerous informal occasions, for example during breakfast and lunch, when I was able to gather information on both teachers' and pupils' perspectives and experiences. I also formally interviewed the Principal, some Area Managers, and a sample of second year students, and gave simple questionnaires to the majority of other students. I was in the college for a total of about 225 hours spread over 29 days, including attendance at two staff development days. What follows is thus the result of a period of 'compressed ethnography', with all the strengths and weaknesses of such a research strategy.

Gaining access to conduct research at the CTC was not straightforward, and I have written elsewhere (Walford 1991a) about the way in which I was eventually given permission – the important points to relate here are that neither teachers nor students were consulted, and the Principal herself was initially very cautious about the extent of access to be granted. At first, I was mainly allocated to be with hand-picked teachers but, as the term continued, trust developed and I was able to negotiate access with other teachers as well. All of the teachers who were asked agreed to be observed and, although I would have preferred it to have been otherwise, most of them were asked only on the same day as being observed, some with only a few minutes' warning. I realized only after I had left that I had missed seeing two of the teachers teaching, and I am sure that they too would have agreed to my presence. For the first half of the term I adopted the strategy of following designated teachers or students for the day, but for the second half of the term I became more selective in the groups and teachers I observed. As the term progressed I gradually became more friendly with members of staff and with students, and they became more trusting of me. Having a 'resident researcher' in the college over the whole term meant that it was difficult for staff and students to keep up an artificial front, even had they wished to.

As the research period was not extensive, what I observed was necessarily selective, and certain activities were bound to have been influenced by my presence. I have tried to give some indication of the atmosphere of the college by including some cameos at the head of some of the sections in this chapter and the next. These have been reconstructed from tape-recorded notes made during the research, and aim to give some examples of day-to-day activities that I observed.

It has to be remembered that this account is already an historical one; the college will have changed even by the time this book is published. I was conducting research in the CTC in the first term of its second year of operation. The staff was small and all the students were aged between 11 and 13. The 'middle-school' atmosphere of that term may have been modified dramatically by the influx of the first post-16 year and another first year intake due in September 1990. Nevertheless, the organizational structures and cultural expectations forged in the early years will structure the shape of later events for both students and the college. This is a record of the workings of the CTC at that time, but it is also a guide to its future.

An ordinary school?

Wednesday 11 October 1989

The modern languages room I am in is arranged with the 'front' on the longest side of the room facing the windows. Six lines of four special student desks are set out in three blocks such that students face each other sitting sideways on to the 'front'. Under a flap in each of these desks is a tape-recorder/player system connected to the master console which enables students to work at their own pace through tapes or take part in teacher-paced activities.

The teacher lets in the group of twenty-two first year students, settles them down, collects homework. Four haven't done it. All are able to negotiate another day to do so. The main topic for the lesson is number work, and today the students don't use the tape system at all. Instead, they use a standard French textbook course and work-sheets to play bingo, sort out number crosswords, and unscramble written numbers. In pairs they play a treasure island game where 'treasure' is hidden in a numbered square on a map, and they have to ask each other in French if a chosen square is correct. The lesson ends with a quick 'Simon Says' game of sitting, standing, putting hands on heads and so on as appropriate. Students leave with smiles on their faces. The teacher explains to me that there was not as much oral work as usual, but that it had been a fairly typical lesson for that age group.

Most newspaper and media discussion of City Technology Colleges has concentrated on those aspects which differ from most maintained secondary schools. The unusual and the different make good news copy, while that which is familiar does not. However, in order to give an understanding of Kingshurst CTC, and in part to act as a counterbalance to media discussion, I first wish to describe those aspects of Kingshurst that it has in common with most other British secondary schools. I shall start with a description of the organizational structure.

For students, the basic organizational block is the tutor group. There are eight mixed ability tutor groups in each of the first two years. It is the intention that each group will stay together for much of the students' careers at the college. The tutor groups are designated by the surname of the tutor, and the individual tutor retains the same group of students as they move from year to year. Tutors are at the front line in terms of dealing with students' problems, absences, discipline and so on, and are expected gradually to build strong relationships with the children in the group and with their parents or guardians as well.

The school day is divided into fixed times during which set subjects are taught by specialist teachers. For most of these lessons the children move from their own tutor group room to another classroom, where they will line up outside the door before being allowed to enter by the teacher. They are usually allowed to choose their own seats within the classroom, but may be allocated specific places on the decision of the teacher. In most cases a group of children is alone with one adult in a classroom for the whole of this fixed time. Within the lesson one of the participants has a very high level of control over all the others. At the CTC that person is always the teacher, who will expect and obtain silence when requested (but not necessarily immediately), will control students' movements, organize their work activities, stop them eating or drinking, and restrict their use of language. Children's appearance, clothing, behaviour and attitudes may be commented upon and criticized at any time by the teacher with no reciprocal rights being given to the children. The work that children do both inside the classroom and outside is set by the teacher and is subject to evaluation (sometimes in front of other children) by that teacher. When the teacher wishes to talk to the class, all others are expected to interrupt whatever they are doing and listen.

All of this can be found in many schools throughout Britain and the western world but with, of course, great variation in the degree of control that individual teachers have over pupils' activities. Within many schools and classrooms, children are also shouted at and verbally abused, made to feel small, ignorant or unwanted. They are told they are nosey, or rude, or liars. The teacher acts as chief prosecutor, judge and jury over what is deemed wrongful behaviour – and sometimes gets it wrong. Additionally the whole group is sometimes punished for the wrong-doings of one of its members – an activity which, if those involved were other than children, would have civil rights groups enraged.

I know of no school where the activities listed in the last paragraph do not occur, and they occurred at Kingshurst CTC as well. However, they were certainly not nearly as common at Kingshurst as they are in many other schools and, as I shall make clear later, the overall atmosphere is very friendly and positive. Nevertheless, the fundamental hierarchical relationship between teacher and pupil is taken for granted within the CTC as in most other schools.

It is also worth remembering that, at the time of my research, the CTC had as pupils a mixture of boys and girls aged 11–13. Girls and boys making friends and breaking them, trying out (but often being deeply embarrassed about) friendships with the opposite sex, gradually forming their own moral codes and testing them against those of others. Girls and boys becoming ill or accidentally injuring themselves; having epileptic fits or coming to terms with the death of a parent. Girls and boys interested in football and swimming, pop music and *Neighbours*; some who spend their time making toy models, and others who prefer to hang around the town centre in the evenings with their friends. Some were involved in petty theft, others had a parent already convicted of a more major crime. Some lived in affluent homes, others on the poverty line. Some were in single parent families, others in reconstituted families and others still with their own parents.

Schooling, whether it be in a CTC or anywhere else, is only a part of being an 11–13 year old, yet all of these external factors influence the child and often that child's work and behaviour in school. In Britain it is generally accepted that the teacher has responsibilities for the overall welfare of the child as well as that of intellectual growth, and helping children to grow was as much a part of the CTC as it is for any good school. At the CTC as elsewhere, teachers deal with a flow of personal problems and delights from children which often impinge directly upon the best-planned lessons.

An extraordinary school?

What, then, of the differences between Kingshurst CTC and most other schools? An outside observer is often able to see organizational features which are too much a part of the 'accepted reality' for insiders to see. I hope to indicate some of these features through looking at a 'typical day' at the CTC, but first it is worth emphasizing the very great architectural and design differences between the CTC and most other schools.

The CTC was designed to provide a pleasant working environment for both staff and students. The uniformly dull row of standard boxes entered from a long corridor, as found in most schools, has been replaced by rooms of varying shapes, sizes and designs. There are no long corridors. Instead, the stairways open on to variously sized entrance spaces, often with adjoining social areas with comfortable chairs, a computer terminal and large potted artificial plants. Each teaching room has its own simple colour scheme, with some co-ordination between the colours of the furniture, walls, carpeting and blinds. Everywhere is carpeted with hard-wearing but attractive carpet tiles, arranged in colourful patterns, to match or contrast with the wall colours. Expensive vertical slat blinds are provided for most rooms in an appropriate colour. Each teaching room has its own internal telephone, television, video-recorder and at least one computer.

There is no standard school furniture – most of it would look equally at home in a business office or industrial laboratory. There are no standard hard school chairs. Apart from the stools in laboratories and some plastic stacking chairs, the majority have padded seats and backs. They look and feel comfortable. Tables are non-standard and differ in colour and type between rooms. They are as likely to be arranged in hexagons as straight lines. Computer areas are supplied with office standard swivel chairs, and social areas are scattered with colourful and relaxing low seating as found in many waiting-rooms and offices. Practically everything still looks new and well looked after. The main visible difference between the CTC and an office block is that most of the walls of the rooms and corridors are filled with colourful expanses of children's work. In all my time there I saw no graffiti anywhere and not a single name or mark written on a desk or bench. The only deliberate damage that I saw was to some of the wall light fittings, which were at child height and of a temptingly vulnerable design.

The college has an open and homely feel. Some of the classrooms further imitate offices in having glass walls through which those passing in the corridor can look. The lavatories for students are positioned within the teaching block, and open on to a short corridor in the same way as any other room. They are bright, clean and decorated to exactly the same standard as are those for staff. There are no cloakrooms, so students leave their coats in their tutor group's room. This has the disadvantage of forcing the students to carry books and other property around with them in bags, but has the benefit of making the form room more truly a 'home' room. Perhaps most important of all, the whole college is always pleasantly warm – sometimes even too hot!

A day at the CTC

The longer school day is one of the major organizational differences between Kingshurst CTC and practically all other schools.

On a research day during the dark winter mornings, I would arrive at about 8.00 am to find the college in a blaze of light. Some of the teachers and students were just arriving, but some of the students had been there from 7.30 am or earlier. Most of the students are not allowed into the main part of the college until 8.20 am, but all can gather in the 'shopping mall' entrance foyer and some have jobs to do which allow them into other areas and to use the computers. Teachers gather in the staff-room for the first of many cups of filtered coffee and for 'briefing', which starts at 8.10 am. This is a time when staff can give and receive general news and information about the day – who is visiting the college, what tutors need to ask their groups to do, plans for the next few days and so on. It is usually taken by the Principal, or the Director of Administration and Finance if she is elsewhere, and attended by all teaching and technical support staff.

For the students, the day starts at 8.20 am when they have to be in their tutor group rooms for registration. With 367 students in 16 groups, these teaching groups varied in size from 21 to 24. Much has been made of the benefits of the college's computerized registration system, but teachers frequently joked that they would welcome back the old written registers – no fuss, no bother, done instantly. The morning and afternoon registration was done by each tutor using the IBM networked into every classroom. The first name of each student was called in alphabetical order of surname irrespective of gender, and a keystroke replaced the mark of a red pen. In some lessons later in the day teachers used a simple written class list and pen to check who was there – and it took less time! A further irony is that for legal and safety reasons, the CTC is required to print a copy of the register as soon as possible after the computerized check-in. To me, it seemed that the main benefit of the system was that all staff were forced to become familiar with the networked computer system, and that having a computer in each classroom throughout the college sometimes changed teaching styles.

Most school days at the CTC are divided into six one-hour sessions grouped in twos. The first two run from 8.25 am until 10.25 am, but it is an indication of the relaxed atmosphere of the college that there are no bells to mark any of the timings during the day. These first two lessons are followed by a tutor group, year or school assembly, and then breakfast. Breakfast is one of the pleasant innovations of the college. A choice is given of a simple hot or cold breakfast with milk or fruit juice. Students pay for each breakfast through a ticket system. As they have now been out of bed for some hours, most children take breakfast, but some prefer to bring a snack instead. This is an administrative blessing, as the inadequate size of the eating area might not otherwise have coped with everyone in the time available. The second two one-hour periods started at 11.05 am and went on until 1.05 pm. During the fifty-minute lunch break that followed, students either ate their own snacks in the hall or had a choice of hot or cold meals in the dining-room. Pressure on space in the dining-hall was again such that tutor groups were assigned to early or late positions in the never-ending queue for food. About 35 per cent of children received free lunches.

One of the most important features of both the breakfast and lunch breaks was that students were allowed to remain inside the college and had access to all the classrooms and social areas. They could use the computers to send and read messages, to play a wide variety of computer games and even, occasionally, to do some academic work and word processing. The Doomsday survey was freely available on video-disk and was often used, or at least played with. As every classroom had a television with full video facilities, students were also able to watch *Neighbours* or whatever else was available during the break-times. These televisions were well used but not, I judged, addictively.

The second registration period at 1.55 pm was usually followed by two more lessons until home time at 4.00 pm. On Wednesdays the afternoon was given over to two of three enrichment periods and the day was lengthened until 4.30 pm. On Friday the last lesson was cut, and students were free to leave at 3.00 pm. It is important to emphasize that although students were free to leave at 4.00 pm on most days, and most did do so, it was not uncommon to have students still using the computing facilities of the college until the early evening. Again, most of this was playing computer games, but some was more directly work orientated.

During their lessons the students should have been set three pieces of homework, each to last them about half an hour. They usually received two or three, and parents had to sign their children's diaries to say that they had seen what homework had been set and that it had been done. As I shall explain later, some students complained that homework often took them far longer than it should have done, for little allowance was usually made to take account of the wide range of abilities.

The staff

Tuesday 12 December 1989

It's lunch-time and I'm in the staff-room. It's a long, rather narrow room, with windows along one of the long sides. It is carpeted and furnished to the same standard as the rest of the college. The low comfortable chairs are of exactly the same type as are scattered round the students' social areas. The carpet and vertical slat blinds are the same as found elsewhere. The room could easily serve as a classroom, just as many of the classrooms could do duty as a staff-room.

At one end of the room are the nests of trays for teachers' letters and messages, a sink and two filter coffee machines. Most days fresh milk is available, but on others powdered milk suffices. Teachers' cups and mugs seem to get lost in the same way as in other schools, but a spare cup can usually be found. At the other end of the room is a photocopying machine with a totally ignored notice on the wall saying that only twelve copies of anything were allowed. Along the long wall opposite the window are a few cupboards, some union notice boards, other notice boards (including a prominent 'No smoking' sign), the timetable and a white board. Two computers and a printer are on a table in front of the notice boards. At the moment the top of the white board has the message: 'This is the place to be' followed by a teacher's name, which is what a national newspaper reporter quoted him as saying in an article on the CTC a few days earlier.

Although it is lunch-time, the room is not very busy. Two of the secretaries are intermittently watching *Neighbours* on the television, while two of the teachers are playing a golfing game on one of the computers. It strikes me that I had just seen students enjoying exactly the same relaxations on some of the various screens scattered throughout the college. Two more teachers are reading newspapers or magazines. A knock at the door. 'Come in!', shouts one of the teachers without moving. Two girls come in: 'Is Mr X here?' 'You can see he's not, sorry.' Another knock comes a minute later. A further teacher has just come in and opens the door: 'Yes?' 'Could I see Miss Y?' 'Can Paul Davies see Miss Y?' he shouts across. Yes, he can.

The college has a low pyramid structure for staff with three organizational levels – Principal, Area Manager, and teaching staff. There are no other permanently designated positions of special responsibility within the hierarchy, but all staff are expected to take extra responsibilities on a temporary basis as required. It is anticipated that the responsibilities of both Area Managers and other teachers will change over time both because there is a need for this in such a rapidly expanding college and because change brings with it new ideas and challenges for the individual staff.

It is an indication of the expectation of continual and rapid change that the Staff Handbook is produced in the form of an A5 loose-leaf binder, with updates at least once a term. In October 1989, the staff list contained forty-one names and included in order: Principal, Director of Administration and Finance, Industrial and Commercial Liaison Officer, Personal Assistant to the Principal, four secretaries, four technicians, two maintenance/security people, six Area Managers and twenty-one other teachers. All staff are listed in this rather unusual order with full first names and surnames without any titles, thus giving the impression of all staff being equally valued and avoiding any stress on gender in nomenclature. Ordinary teaching staff are listed in alphabetical order with their academic teaching subject.

The number of staff has gradually increased with the growth of student numbers, but about two-thirds of those employed in late 1989 had been at the college since September 1988 or before. Amongst the twenty-seven teaching staff there is a range of age and experience. All are graduates. All but one have a teaching qualification, three through the BEd route and the remainder through postgraduate training. There is one member of staff with a doctorate and four with MA degrees. Four of the staff came to the college as probationary teachers, twenty were previously teaching in state-maintained schools (including four at the comprehensive where Valerie Bragg was previously Head), and one came from a college of further education. Only one of the teachers was previously teaching in the private sector, and that was at the United World College in Singapore. Two of the staff were from Birmingham's voluntary aided grammar school system, the King Edward's Schools, Birmingham. About six of the staff have had substantial experience in industry, including one who moved directly from industry to the college and one of the probationary teachers, who trained to teach as a mature student. None of the staff was previously teaching in schools within the catchment area of the CTC, and only one now lives within that catchment area, even though several have moved from other parts of the country to work at the CTC. Some teachers have retained their membership of unions such as AMMA and NAS/UWT and, unlike at Nottingham CTC, union membership is not discouraged. The Principal is a member of the Secondary Heads Association. The CTC also has a small pool of regular supply staff, and several peripatetic music staff. At the time of the research there were sixteen male and eleven female permanent teaching staff. The staff includes some probationary teachers, who were appointed because of their perceived enthusiasm, new ideas and recent knowledge.

After the initial major appointment of Principal had been made, the governing body delegated the authority to appoint staff to the Principal, who has always been able to choose between a very wide list of candidates for posts. Advertisements for Area Managers, for example, brought hundreds of applications – in one case over 1,000. One block advertisement for 10 subject teaching staff brought over 700 applications. The applicants included those with previous experience in polytechnics and universities as well as colleges of further education, state-maintained and private schools. A good number of students in training had also applied. Very few Heads are privileged to have such a large field of applicants to draw from, and it would be a poor Head indeed who was not able to choose staff with an impressive range of abilities, interests and teaching skills.

The precise criteria used in selection of staff are always difficult to articulate. On interview, Valerie Bragg emphasized that, as she had been a Head before, she was not looking for anything very different from what she had looked for in her last school. Her appointment of four teachers from her previous school would tend to confirm that statement. She had aimed for a mix of staff, in terms of age, gender and experience, but in all of them had looked for what she called flair, ideas, creativity, imagination and originality. One interesting point is that, for most of the jobs, experience of technology or computing skills was not a criterion used – what mattered to her was that they were willing to learn. The result of this policy was that, in practice, the vast majority of staff had hardly any computing experience before appointment. Much more important than experience of technology was a willingness to become involved with teaching based on a practical approach with a lot of group-work and cross-curricular activities.

These first twenty-seven appointments (twenty-eight including the Principal) indicate that some of the fears voiced by the Association of Metropolitan Authorities in their document opposing the CTC initiative (AMA 1987: 6) may have been unjustified. AMA was concerned about the problem of teacher supply in 'shortage' subject areas such as maths, physics and CDT, and the possible effect of teacher deployment in the locality of the CTC. The booklet gave an example of one 'medium-sized authority in the West Midlands' (presumably *not* Solihull) where in December 1986 there were seven unfilled vacancies in mathematics, two real and four hidden vacancies in computer studies, two vacancies in business studies, two schools with no physics specialists and four where the physics teachers lacked expertise in vital areas of the new curriculum. It was thought that a CTC would produce further local shortage of teachers in these and similar subjects and that nearby schools would be unable to maintain a full curriculum. There was also a concern that highly experienced local teachers in other subjects might be attracted into the CTCs by higher pay and better facilities.

The previous appointments of the twenty-eight teaching staff in post at Kingshurst CTC in December 1989 suggest that the college has had no effect on the staffing situation of schools in the catchment area, as all of the teachers had been appointed from outside. Only four were previously teaching in Solihull or Birmingham, including two from the King Edward's grammar schools. While the vast majority of staff have come from the state-maintained sector, what seems to have happened is that high-quality staff have been attracted into this somewhat depressed, predominantly working-class, urban area. It is unlikely that many of them would have been attracted into neighbouring secondary schools for jobs at the same level. Thus, while there has been a loss of staff from the maintained sector to the CTC, this loss has occurred from over a wide area (except the five from the Principal's former school and the two from King Edward's grammar schools), and the flow has been from mixed and middle-class areas and schools to a predominantly working-class estate. Informal conversations with teachers confirmed that most of the staff regarded their previous school to have been in a more socially mixed and desirable area.

As the college is a registered independent school it is not tied to nationally imposed salary scales and, like any other independent school, can pay staff whatever it likes. However, once the CTCs have reached their equilibrium size, the DES funding for current expenditure will be based upon funding made available by LEAs for schools in similar areas. This means that the overall salary bill cannot be significantly higher than that of a comparably sized LEA school unless additional funding can be found. Kingshurst does not follow the Baker Scale but has a very simple salary structure with two broad continuous salary bands – one for Area Managers and another for all other teachers. In practice this simply means that each of the two bands has a top and bottom point and teachers can be paid anything between these two points. The bottom of the teachers' scale is very slightly higher than the minimum for state school teachers and rises to very slightly above the top salary available for a classroom teacher. The crucial decision as to where individual teachers should be positioned within either band is made by the Principal according to the teacher's experience and previous salary.

In the light of arguments about attracting specialist staff away from state-maintained schools it is important to note that the Principal specifically pointed out that the position within the salary band is not related to the subject taught. To do so would be against the general philosophy of the college whereby all subject areas are equally valued. As individual staff salaries are confidential, I was unable actually to check what teachers in shortage subject areas were being paid. However, as the college was inundated with applications from science, art and design and CDT specialists it is most unlikely that, as a group, they would be paid more than other teachers at the college.

The other most important differences between the Kingshurst salaries and state school salaries (and, indeed, most private school salaries) is that increments are given on the basis of performance, and no teacher automatically gains an increment at the end of each year. Performance is ultimately judged by the Principal, with some teachers getting no increment at all and the size of the increments varying widely. All staff do automatically receive a yearly increase in salary to account for inflation. For the first two years of the CTC's life, staff have also been given a small Christmas bonus, but this is not part of the regular salary and at Christmas 1989, when I was in the college, staff did not know whether or not they would be getting this bonus until the pay slips arrived.

Some of the extra funding necessary for slightly higher than maintained schools' salaries and for performance-related pay is given specially by one of the sponsors – Lucas Industries – for this purpose. At the point I was doing research at the CTC, sponsor-ship money was also being used to cover the costs of auxiliary technical and secretarial staff.

All staff are appraised every year on a top-down basis using a simple staff pre-appraisal discussion form. Most teaching staff are appraised by Area Managers, who are themselves appraised by the Principal. The system in use resulted from the ideas of one of the early working parties established before the college actually opened and considerable consultation with various industrial sponsors, unions and others. Its aim is to adopt some current ideas about appraisal from industry without needless complexity. There is an attempt to separate this regular appraisal, which is about a member of staff's personal development plans, from salary increments and performance-related pay. The appraisal is thus conducted in about April of each year and performance-related pay is given in July. Performance-related pay is separate from salary increments and is based on extra targets set by teachers themselves in conjunction with the relevant Area Manager. Performance-related pay is given on a year-by-year basis and is linked to activities over and above the teacher's normal job.

Any judgements about the quality of the staff appointed and of their teaching abilities are necessarily subjective, and I do not pretend to be an expert at judging the effectiveness of teaching. However, during the term I observed a large number of lessons, and saw none that was 'bad'. All of the teachers I observed (often with only minutes' notice) appeared to have planned their lessons. They knew what they wanted to do and what they wanted their students to achieve in the time available. Lessons were structured and ordered and students actually did (most of) the work required of them. Some of the staff would probably be rated as exceptional teachers by any independent observer.

Several attempts have been made to try to stop barriers form-ing between teaching and other staff. This shows itself in many minor, although significant, ways. For example, where they have special skills, some of the technicians are involved in actual teach-ing of small groups of students. They are expected to be obeyed by students in the same way as teaching staff and have the right to give detentions or merit marks as deemed appropriate. At the CTC the traditional caretaker is replaced by two maintenance/security people, and the well-known ways that caretakers have of obtaining respect are extended to the giving of merit marks. They also tutor some enrichments. Other ways in which integration is encouraged include the staff common-room being available and used by secretarial and technical staff as well as teachers and joint meetings of staff. For example, there is a full staff meeting once each term which includes all full-time staff, and the Christmas staff party in 1989 was open to all full and part-time staff and partners and had well over 100 people attending.

Although the AMA did not recognize the problem of a dearth of appropriately qualified and experienced technical staff in its booklet (AMA 1987), it is probably in this area that local shortages are more likely to result from the CTC than in other areas. Technical staff are less well paid than teaching staff and those with knowledge of new technology are in great demand. They are also probably less likely to move into a new district to take up a job than are teachers. At the CTC there had already been some turnover of technical staff into more highly paid jobs elsewhere and three of the four current technicians had come from the local area (although not necessarily the CTC catchment area). Secretarial staff had also come from the local area, but here competition was not as fierce as for trained technical staff.

There are two more members of the CTC staff to be considered. The first of these is the Director of Administration and Finance, whose main role is something similar to that of a school Bursar. However, the title of Director of Administration and Finance indicates that the role is wider than that of most Bursars in private schools, and includes overall control of many everyday administrative matters that are often delegated to senior teaching staff in other schools. Thus, for example, he is even responsible for ensuring that teachers cover the classes of absent or otherwise occupied colleagues – an unpopular task usually delegated to one of the Deputy Heads. The current holder of the post has never been a teacher, but has come from industry and commerce to the job. However, he is clearly a prominent member of the college's senior management team and his high status within the hierarchy is illustrated by his taking of daily briefing in the Principal's absence.

The final member of staff to be considered here is the Industrial and Commercial Liaison Officer, who works on reduced hours four days each week. The present officer is actually in semi-retirement, following a senior position in one of the CTC's sponsoring companies, but has a major task of liaising with current and potential business sponsors and supporters. Part of this task is

chasing donations already promised to the CTC through covenants, as not all of the sponsors have been as regular in their
pledged donations as might be hoped. The names of sponsors on
the 'Sponsors and Supporters' notice board in the entrance foyer to
the CTC have occasionally been changed to take into account
particularly tardy payers. Equally important is the task of ensuring
that sponsors are kept aware of what the CTC is doing and are
invited to, and taken care of at, all of the various public college
functions. Whether it be the visitors' day during Project Week, the
termly dramatic production, a concert or any other special event,
all sponsors are invited to attend and give special treatment if they
do so. As in business, it is recognized that goodwill has to be
worked at, and may lessen if not rewarded in some way.

Another part of this job is developing new contacts with
industry and commerce. There are visits from industrialists to the
college and by teachers to industry. For example, all of the senior
teaching staff have been on three-week management training
courses designed by sponsors for their own managers. As the pupils
get older there will also be a need for work experience placements
for them. At the time of the research it seemed that there had been
sufficient promises of places for all students to have such placements, but changing those promises into reality was expected to be
a further time-consuming task.

Life in the fast track

Wednesday 18 October 1989

It's now nearly 10.00 pm. I've just left the CTC, having arrived there
this morning at 8.00 am. Being a Wednesday, the normal school
lessons finished at 4.30 pm, but lessons started again at 7.00 pm for a
special parents' lessons evening, where parents experience something of what it is like to be a student at the CTC. The evening
started with a brief introduction in the crowded hall. Parents had
previously been given the chance to opt out of PE and drama if they
wished, but no other choices were allowed, and we all set out for
our allocated lessons. I pretended to be a parent in both of the two
forty-five-minute lessons. The first was Spanish, where I re-
experienced the embarrassment of my linguistic ineptitude. It was
friendly enough, but actually being expected to reply to questions
reminded me forcefully of childhood fears.

The second lesson was economic awareness, where the main aim was to let us discover that division of labour led to greater efficiency. This was a larger group than before and we were divided into four groups of five or six. Each group was to select a manager and a quality controller and the rest were to be production workers. I had watched the children make this sort of decision many times, but it seemed rather more difficult with people who had only just met – I think we chose unwisely! The task set was to produce as many three-page booklets as possible during each ten-minute 'day' and for these to be of high enough quality to 'sell' them to the 'buyers'. The raw materials (paper) had to be 'bought' and equipment (scissors, rulers, glue and pens) 'hired'. The paper then had to be cut to size, three sheets glued together and the word 'PRODUCTION' written on the front. A balance sheet was drawn up at the end of each 'day' and the results of the four groups compared. All four groups would quickly have been declared bankrupt! It was a most peculiar experience to be involved in the frenzied production process, and to have some of our products rejected as not of a high enough standard by the buyers! But it was enjoyable, and did push home the message that good planning and greater division of labour would certainly have helped in this case. There was no time to discuss the more negative features of such work processes, but we were assured that these would be included in a real set of lessons.

After coffee and biscuits, parents gathered again in the hall and Mrs Bragg answered a succession of questions on various aspects of the CTC. Several of the parents thanked her and the teachers for the evening, but most of the questions ranged widely: Can we have a parents' drama club? What was the sixth form going to be like? Is there going to be a PTA? Can we have some lockers for children's belongings? How about a summer uniform? Why are so many people opposed to the CTC? Could we get a Zebra crossing? Can we have a gate at the back of the school field? And so on, until nearly 10.00 pm.

Teaching staff often joked about working 'in the fast track'. It was one of the Principal's oft-used expressions, and one which the staff used when additional pressures were put on them. Building a new school from nothing is certainly both a marvellous opportunity and challenge, but is also simply a great deal of very hard work. Moreover, building a new school is not made any easier where the school is the first of its kind and constantly in the eye of the national media, and where there is a context of economic and political uncertainty. The City Technology College, Kingshurst, has had to live through gradual changes in government policy towards the CTCs and has had continually to fight for sufficient additional funding from the DES to enable it to carry out the task set for it by itself and by government. This has meant that the funding agreement between the CTC and the DES has been through nine revisions: there has been a continual state of uncertainty over future capital and current expenditure. The current idea from the DES that CTCs should be funded on the same basis as LEA schools is far from what was expected in 1987, and the additional funding necessary to run a high technology school has had to be fought for. 'Life in the fast track' means setting out for the future with the planning for that future still incomplete, in the hope that there will be sufficient flexibility in that planning to allow for all eventualities.

'Life in the fast track' can also be associated with the sheer number of activities with which staff are involved and the public visibility of everything that the CTC does. In the single term that I was there the college had an informal inspection by HMIs, was filmed by BBC television for about two weeks and taped by BBC World Service for a further two days, was visited by dozens of individual VIPs, had a general open day for more than 100 sponsors, supporters and guests during the students' Project Week, produced a full-scale musical production for three nights, an orchestral concert for another night and dealt with an 'informal' visit from HRH Prince Philip. Apart from innumerable comments and small stories in practically all national newspapers during that term, the college also had major articles about its activities in the *Financial Times*, the *Daily Telegraph* and the *Times Educational Supplement*. In amongst all this, of course, not only did the present students have to be taught, sports fixtures organized and day-to-day problems overcome, but also the third-year curriculum had to be developed, a new first year attracted through advertisements and leaflets, and a whole new post-16 programme of BTEC First and National Diplomas and International Baccalaureate negotiated. It was little wonder that when I asked teachers about the new college buildings that were being constructed, they said that they had not had any time to see what they were going to be like!

Multiple roles and duties for teachers are an accepted part of the job in all schools, but the high visibility of the college, the sheer number of different activities shared amongst a relatively small staff, and the college's own stress on high quality, meant that pressures on these teachers were extremely heavy.

4

Resources and the curriculum

Funding and support

The original Department of Education and Science booklet outlining the CTC scheme stated that 'the Government is working with interested individuals and organisations to establish with financial assistance from the Department of Education and Science a network of City Technology Colleges in urban areas' (DES 1986: 2) and that 'the promoters will make a substantial contribution towards the cost' (1986: 4). However, as indicated in Chapter 1, industry has been unprepared to finance the CTCs at anything near the originally expected level. Rather than the DES giving financial 'assistance', it has become by far the major funder, and the Treasury has been forced to pay for the greater part of the building and renovation programme for the network of colleges as well as for ongoing recurrent expenditure.

In the entrance foyer to The CTC at Kingshurst there is a prominently displayed list of 'Sponsors and Supporters'. Hanson plc and Lucas Industries are given pride of place at the top of the board, and a further fifty-one organizations are listed in three columns of seventeen. This additional funding from industry and commerce, although important and very welcome, has not been as great as many of those outside the college believe. The Hanson plc's initial gift of £1 million went directly to Solihull Council in return for a long lease on the Kingshurst site and buildings. Up until the end of 1989, the total additional funding given or pledged by all of these other sponsors and supporters was a little under £2 million. Thirty-three sponsors had given cash donations or cash equivalent donations of equipment, but the range of generosity was considerable. Most of the support has been given in the form of covenants over four years such that they attract tax relief, with total amounts pledged ranging from a low of £125 over five years to several gifts in the hundreds of thousands. One of the important tasks of the Industrial Liaison Officer is to ensure that companies actually keep to their pledged levels of support. Where the direct support has not been in the form of a covenanted gift, it has sometimes been in direct gifts of equipment. Thus a car manufacturer provided a car for both the Principal and the Director of Administration and Finance, one engineering company has provided tools, while another has given an expensive CNC lathe on semi-permanent loan. Hanson plc provided a set of electronic typewriters, and there have been donations of (or heavy discount on) computers and computer software.

Support from the DES has also not been as generous as is generally believed. It has now been publicly admitted by the City Technology Colleges Trust that the DES woefully underestimated the costs involved in setting up the colleges; obtaining adequate funding from the DES has been a continuing battle. In order to justify the grant from the DES, the CTC has been forced to itemize all significant expenditure needs within each subject area. The result is that, while the CTC is well provided for in some areas, it lacks equipment in others; in only a few areas is provision actually lavish.

Staff as a resource

Friday 27 October 1989

It's a double Art and Design lesson with a group of twenty-two second year students. At first we are in the large design room on the second floor. As I arrive I am surprised to see two girls sitting on desks – something that I have not seen before in lessons. More of the students do the same, and I recognize that the teacher is going to talk to them there. They sit in a tight group on stools and on the tables so that they can clearly see the examples that the teacher shows them. They have done some illustrated lettering for homework, and he is showing them the best examples, asking them what they thought was good about them, and explaining what he considered to be the best features. Some are extremely imaginative and of high quality, with letters formed from animals, people and various inanimate objects.

The students had started work on their own designs for highly personalized folders the week before. The teacher just tells them to get on with it, and ask for his help if they need it. At this point, the lesson becomes very difficult to observe! Some students work in this room using paints, inks or pencils, but a few go off to the dark-room to develop and print photographs, while others go down to the CDT room. Two teachers run their sessions in parallel so that two groups of students can use all the facilities of the two main craft, art and design areas. Students do not have to ask permission to go elsewhere, and some of this second group have decided to come up to use the design room. I wander down to the craft area, where some students are cutting out clay letters which will then be vacuum moulded with thin plastic, others are making clay pots, or using craft equipment. Back upstairs, some students are printing their designs on to fabric which will be used to cover their folders. Two students from yet another class have now come in to use the computer and are busy with LOGO.

The whole atmosphere is one of purposeful and productive activity. At the end of the session, the students know that they have got to be able to show that they have accomplished something worthwhile, and they are left to make their own decisions as to how to use their time. The lesson has a very relaxed feel. Students natter to each other and enjoy themselves, but they also get a great deal of work done. The vast majority clearly also want to produce something that is good, rather than just acceptable. There is very little mucking around, and it is rare for any of the teachers to have to discipline a student. Students use the equipment sensibly, and frequently with real flair and imagination. I wander around, observe discreetly, talk to students about their work, and the two hours quickly pass.

The most important resource in any school is its staff. At the time of the research there were twenty-eight teachers at the college (including the Principal) and 367 children, which gave an overall pupil/teacher ratio of 13.1. This is about mid-way between the 1988 average for secondary schools in England of 15.4 and the average for independent schools of 11.3 (DES 1989a). Although it is clearly a better ratio than that within the average secondary school, the college serves an area with special needs, and it is always the case that a newly established school is granted extra teachers to deal with advance planning, and to staff the full curriculum while pupil numbers grow to a steady state. Once the steady state has been reached the intention is that the DES will give sufficient funding only to achieve the national average ratio. Any additional staff will have to be financed by private funding. Overall, at the time of the research the pupil/teacher ratio was generous, but not excessively so. In terms of size of class actually taught, the 1988 average for all secondary school classes taught on a particular census day was 20.7. Taking only those classes taught by one teacher, the average size of class was 19.9, while for classes of children mainly aged under 16, the average was 22.4 (DES 1989a). Against these figures the CTC's average class size of 23.6 for the first year and 22.25 for the second year do not look over generous. As the CTC's attendance rate was high, the size of classes as taught differed little from the national average. Indeed, as there were falling school rolls within the CTC's catchment area, many pupils in most nearby LEA schools would have been taught in smaller classes than those at the CTC.

Where the college has a greater advantage over LEA secondary schools is with its non-teaching staff. Four technicians and two maintenance/security people, all of whom had very flexible job definitions, and five staff dealing with administration and finance, is far greater than would be allocated to a similarly sized new LEA school. It is worth noting that while the special situation that Kingshurst found itself in as the first CTC certainly necessitated extra secretarial and administrative staff, the DES was unprepared to fund them. Money from sponsors has been used to pay for the extra non-teaching staff that the college requires. Lucas has also provided funding for the Industrial Liaison Officer.

Sponsors not only have provided cash for staffing, but also have been prepared to second their own staff to the college and to provide help and assistance when requested. This donation of specialists' time was of particular importance during the period before the CTC opened. For example, Lucas seconded a manager to work four days per week with the CTC, while other sponsors and supporters provided advisers on technology, computing, accountancy, legal issues, salary structures, management and so on, both as individuals and within Advisory Committees. Since the CTC has opened, this support has continued with both formal and informal contacts between teachers and industrialists within the supporting companies. Sponsors still regularly provide advice if requested to do so, and visit the college. They occasionally give talks to students and take part in teaching. They also act as a resource for the college to draw on for visits and will provide work experience placements for students as the college develops.

Over-resourced?

The public image of the City Technology College, Kingshurst, is of a college bursting with expensive computers, video cameras, and high-technology craft, design and technology equipment; the reality is closer to that of some secondary schools elsewhere than CTC critics would wish to admit. The CTC is undoubtedly well provided for but, with the possible exception of computers, the difference between it and the better-provided maintained schools is not overwhelming.

There are many aspects to information technology, but the one which most commentators are particularly concerned with is that of the number and quality of computers to which pupils have access. In the first year of operation, the CTC made the claim that there was one computer for every two children. While technically correct, this was always an optimistic description of the computing power actually available to students. The main hardware used for teaching and administration was the Novel Token ring network with thirty-two IBM 502s which links every classroom. The other work-horses were thirty-eight Archimedes 310s. In addition to this, there were about three Amstrads, three BBC Masters, and twenty Z88 laptop portables. This computing power was supported by about thirty printers, one colour printer and two laser printers. In practice, however, not all of these computers were actually available to students. The Z88s, for example, were allocated to members of staff for their own use, and some of the IBMs were used only by administrative staff. No further computer hardware was bought for the second year of operation of the college, so there were actually about five or six students per computer at the time of the research. The figure is likely to increase further in the third year of operation of the college, when there will be post-16 students as well as a further 11 year old intake without matching expenditure on new machines.

These figures may be compared with the results of a survey into information technology in schools conducted by the DES in February 1988 (DES 1989b). Its representative sample of secondary schools had an average of 23.2 computers per school and one computer per 32 children. These figures had improved by a factor of about two in the three years since the previous survey. It is noteworthy that there was considerable variation between schools in the level of provision, with 5.1 per cent of secondary schools having more than fifty computers. However, even in these relatively well-provided-for schools, it is unlikely that the quality of the machines matched those of the CTC. Some 41 per cent of computers in LEA schools were BBC Acorns, and another 24 per cent were Acorn Masters. Only 0.6 per cent of the machines were IBM.

The two most important decisions made by the CTC about the computing equipment were that it should be of 'industrial standard' where possible and that it should be available in every classroom rather than being concentrated only in specific computing rooms. It was felt important that students should be able to see teaching and administrative staff using the same sort of equipment and software as students were using themselves, and that they should know that these were of the same type and standard as used in business. Consultation with local industrialists and sponsors led to the purchase of the IBM and Archimedes machines, and also to the adoption of Word Perfect as the standard word-processing package. A Lotus 1-2-3 clone was adopted as the standard spreadsheet. One of the major information technology costs was for the computer networking which connects all the major rooms of the college. This necessitated a high initial investment which will become more worthwhile only as the number of computers increases.

In addition to this computing hardware, the college's information technology resources include several video cameras, a video editing room, satellite television receivers, a stand-alone Doomsday video-disk reader, various CAD lathes and other technology and design equipment. There is a television, satellite link and video-recorder in each classroom, and the college was given twenty-four electronic typewriters by a sponsoring company. The college is well supplied with software for word processing, data bases, spreadsheets, desk-top publishing, and various art and design packages such as Pro-Artisan and Paint.

Earmarked government support for information technology at the CTC was a total of £250,000 over five years, by which point there should be about 1,300 students in the college. This level of funding can be compared with expenditure for LEA schools in 1987/88 (DES 1989b), when the average secondary school spent £4,872 on information technology equipment (£6.48 per pupil). Within these secondary schools, about half of IT funding had come from capitation grants, 20 per cent from other LEA grants, 8 per cent from TVEI and 9 per cent from parent/teacher associations. The sum spent on information technology at the CTC can be seen to be about ten times more than this average, but again the average conceals considerable variation between LEA schools.

The CTC's policy on information technology is that it should be seen as a tool to be used by staff and students as part of their everyday lives. To be able to do this staff need to have direct access to IT wherever they are teaching, such that administrative tasks and teaching can be more effective and efficient. Thus, apart from an introductory course in the first year, IT is not regarded as a separate part of the curriculum. The aim is to use it to 'deepen, broaden and widen' the whole curriculum.

Very few of the teaching staff had IT experience before appointment to the CTC, but the expectation held by everyone was that they would quickly learn. Indeed, the computerized register and administration system, which includes a records of achievement system for students, ensures that all staff must become computer literate. An important part of this learning process occurs through regular Curriculum Area meetings designed to develop staff IT skills and knowledge. All teaching, administrative and technical staff (including the Principal) have these regular timetabled slots each week with the Area Manager for Information Technology. While timetabling does not ensure that it always happens, of course, it does make it far more likely, and these sessions are seen as an important part of in-service training. They vary in structure and may take the form of training in new developments, practice on various packages or discussion. At the time of the research six teachers were taking a Royal Society of Arts modular IT teachers' certificate course. All of the staff were computer literate, and practically all used computers on a regular basis.

These figures can be contrasted with those for LEA secondary schools in February 1988, when only 84 per cent of computer science teachers used microcomputers at least twice a week on average (DES 1989b). While the proportion of teachers in most subjects who used computers at least twice a week was less than 30 per cent, 60 per cent of business studies, 38 per cent of CDT and 34 per cent of music teachers made use of computers to this extent.

Under-resourced?

While the micro-electronic forms of information technology are provided on a more generous scale than in most other secondary schools, the more traditional forms of information technology are not. School libraries gradually grow over the years so, without a massive initial investment, a new school is at a disadvantage compared with older ones. The CTC library was recognized by teachers as being poor. Indeed, when the library was mentioned, it was not infrequent for a teacher to joke 'What library?' At the time of the research the library shelves looked more empty than full, and books were positioned face forward to help fill the space. The range of books was limited, and students often could not find very much in the library about areas that interested them, or which they were trying to research. Any new school will experience similar problems, for it is difficult to justify a large expenditure on reference books which may or may not be used. The lack of older students meant that the more specialized books that they require were not available to act as reference material for younger students.

This lack of books was not restricted to the library. In class, students often had to share textbooks, or use worksheets instead of textbooks. Some class sets of textbooks were available in most subjects, but there were never sufficient sets for all students. The eight parallel classes in each year had to share the various sets of books according to what particular aspect of the subject they were learning. This meant that books were usually given out for specific lessons and then collected in again, rather than being loaned to the students for a longer period. There were no class sets of novels for English.

This lack of equipment exhibited itself in a variety of areas of the curriculum. Subject areas such as music or food technology were well equipped. Music had a good range of keyboards, metalaphones and percussion instruments for class use, while students learning a particular wind, brass or string instrument were loaned instruments on a long-term basis if they could not afford to buy their own. The class instruments were used frequently and for a variety of purposes. In a similar way, the food technology room was well supplied with cookers, microwave ovens and similar everyday equipment, all of which were in regular use. In contrast, the nature of science teaching is that specialist equipment may be used for a particular experiment only a few times each year and cannot be used for a wide variety of tasks. Thus in this second year of opening, the science teachers at the CTC sometimes found themselves in short supply of specific infrequently used items. For example, there were insufficient microscopes for more than one class to use them at any one time. Light boxes had an insufficient range of lenses and prisms to allow students to investigate phenomena fully. Well-established schools have the advantage of a diversity of equipment that has been gradually gathered over the years. It would be difficult to justify buying a mechanical contrivance which may be used only once a year, but its presence gives variety to what can be done.

The shortages in various areas showed clearly when HRH Prince Philip came to the college on an 'informal' visit. The whole visit was very carefully choreographed, and class sizes had to be adjusted so that he would not see that there were insufficient science kits for all the children who were actually timetabled to do science. On that very special occasion, the CTC also borrowed a further set of about twenty micro-computers from one of the sponsors, so that the effect presented was that of a superbly equipped college.

It must be recognized that 1988 was a particularly difficult year for any new school to open. The planning stage for the CTC coincided with the rapid passage of the 1988 Education Reform Act through Parliament, with its proposals for the National Curriculum and its associated testing. At that time, no one knew what the National Curriculum would entail, and the details have only gradually become clear during 1989 and 1990 as the various programmes of study and attainment targets have been developed. The CTC Kingshurst is obliged to follow the 'substance' of the National Curriculum, but it has decided to follow it as closely as possible, which has led to a hiatus in buying books and equipment. It would be foolish to purchase class sets of textbooks at a time when they are likely to be superseded within a year or two, and equally unwise to buy specialist equipment which may not be required.

The college has also been hampered by the way in which the physical building and renovation has been organized. The original intention was to renovate all the old buildings and for there to be very little new building. In practice, this proved impossible and the college has been cramped into just one block for the first two years of its life, while a new extension has been built. The lack of space in the college has been a particular problem in the second year of operation when the number of students doubled without any increase in classrooms. It has presented special difficulties to several of the staff. For example, there was only one designated art-room, which meant that those teaching art and design were forced to use the CDT room, a science laboratory or any other spare room in a make-shift way. The science laboratories had to be fitted out with a non-permanent bench arrangement, which looks very impressive, but is less than perfect in terms of actual teaching. The large CDT room often has two groups using it, sometimes for unrelated subjects such as mathematics. This improved once the new building opened in September 1990, but by then the college had once again doubled in size.

The subject curriculum

According to the original DES booklet of October 1986 (DES 1986: 2), City Technology Colleges were designed 'to provide a broadly-based secondary education with a strong technological element'. The same document gave an illustration of a possible curriculum for years 1 to 3, which suggested that over the three years there might be 25 per cent mathematics and science (including some aspects of technology), 20 per cent design and its realization, 25 per cent humanities and 30 per cent for other courses including business understanding and personal development. It also made clear that cross-curricular themes such as health and environmental education and the development of study skills were to be included within the curriculum. When it is explained that design and its realization includes art and design, CDT and home economics, and that expressive arts are to include music and drama, the proposed curriculum does not look very different from the thrust of the National Curriculum introduced in the 1988

Education Reform Act. However, in October 1986 there were no public plans for any Education Act, and only later was it made clear by Regulation that CTCs would keep to 'the substance' of the National Curriculum – whatever that may mean!

For teachers and students at the CTC, the curriculum is structured through the weekly timetable of twenty-nine hour-long lessons. In the autumn term of 1989 this was divided into the subject areas shown in Table 4.1.

Enrichments are a particular feature of the CTC curriculum, and will be discussed later in this chapter. Two of the three enrichment periods are timetabled on Wednesday afternoons and are actually seventy-five minutes each, while the third is timetabled on Friday morning and is only one hour. All students are timetabled for personal and social education at the same time on Wednesday morning with their form tutors. They also have some additional time with their tutors instead of one of the assemblies. The total timetable thus covers thirty hours.

One of the most noticeable aspects of curriculum as embodied in the timetable is how *little* time is given to science and technology rather than how much. Thus, if we include all of the science, CDT, IT, art and design, and food technology, this accounts for ten of the thirty hours, or 33 per cent in the first year. It actually goes down to 30 per cent in the second year with the loss of the information technology lesson.

Table 4.1 Allocated periods to each subject area

		1st year	2nd year
English and communication	(Eng)	3	3
Mathematical studies	(Ma)	3	3
Science	(Sc)	3	3
Sports sciences	(PE)	1	1
Food technology	(FT)	2	2
Craft, design and technology	(CDT)	2	2
Information technology	(IT)	1	0
Human studies	(HS)	3	3
Business and economic awareness	(Ec)	1	1
Foreign language communication	(ML)	2	3
Design and graphics	(AD)	2	2
Expressive arts	(Mu) + (Dr)	2	2
Personal and social eduction	(PSE)	1	1
Enrichments	(Enr)	3	3

However, describing the curriculum simply in terms of the subject identities gives an inadequate indication of the true coverage of science and technology. In particular, staff would argue that information technology is to be found throughout the curriculum and that students use a variety of different technologies within other subject areas. What at first sight appears to be a simple question of counting lessons denoted as technological subjects becomes a very complicated question of whether using a video camera to record drama should be counted as technological. Moreover, some children may experience more technology than others within the same classes, for while some choose to use word processors to write their essays in an English lesson, others choose to use pen and paper. As described later in this chapter, this is further complicated by optional choices made for the three enrichment lessons each week and the choices made during Project Weeks, when the normal timetable is suspended and students work in groups on their own projects. Assessing the amount of science and technology in the CTC's first and second year curriculum thus relies upon subjective definitions of what should be 'counted', and on the concept of the average child's experience.

The use made of information technology and other scientific and technological equipment is limited by what is available. As has been shown in the last section, while the CTC is well equipped with computers, there is only one IT room which can be used by a whole class, and the remaining computers are scattered around the whole college, usually with two or three to a room. At the time of the research, demand for computing facilities often exceeded supply, and the hunt for a free computer was a recurrent feature of student (and sometimes staff) life.

The familiar curriculum?

Thursday 19 October 1989

English. Before the kids come in the teacher explains to me that this is going to be a dull lesson to watch. The class is going to write a first draft of a story about Aliens. They had spent the last lesson generating ideas and working out essay plans in small groups, and this was going to be the session in which they actually wrote a first draft. They come into the room and find their seats round octagonal tables. The teacher reminds them of what they have been doing, and questions them about the need for characterization in stories. She then announces that they are going to write the story in this lesson. Several of the children become excited at the idea. One asks how long it is to be. She refuses to say, arguing that length is for them to decide, but emphasized that waffle adds nothing to a story and is not required. Can it be written in the first person? Again, it is for them to decide the advantages and disadvantages of such a strategy.

They work for about twenty minutes with hardly a sound. The teacher stops them: 'Put up your hand if you are annoyed that I've stopped you.' All hands go up. 'Okay, carry on, then.' At one point a couple of students from another class come in to use the computer. They ask permission, which is granted, but when the time comes to print out, the noise disturbs the others. They leave after about ten minutes. The teacher checks how people are doing, reads some of the stories, and talks quietly to others. She calls the writing to a halt and reads out sections of three of the stories, indicating how good she thinks they are and why. They are to finish off for homework. Next week they will do a final draft and probably produce a word-processed finished product.

Valerie Bragg has stated at a public Education Management Association meeting that the curriculum in the first two years at the CTC is not exceptional. It departs from what might be expected in any good school in only a few specific areas. On the whole, a range of experienced teachers has been appointed who have created their syllabuses and schemes of work on the basis of what they perceive to be 'best practice' in other schools. As one of the Area Managers explained to me, 'It would be crazy to reinvent the wheel'. For the most part, the curriculum thus follows the same broad areas as other schools, but is modified to take account of the opportunities that the enhanced technological provision affords.

This can be seen through English, for example, where writing skills are developed through discussion of punctuation and paragraphing, verbs and synonyms, much as in other schools. Letters and essays are written as well as newspaper stories and advertisements. There is class reading, and discussion of sections from novels, as well as critique of language use for different audiences. The difference is that more use was made of appropriate technology, in particular word processing, with its advantages of allowing poor writers and spellers to present work well. Students, working in pairs on computers, allowed each to make a real input into the written work of the other in a way that was not easily possible using pen and paper. In English there was also greater use of video than would be possible at most other schools, but this was not used excessively. English is part of a Languages and Communications Curriculum Area which includes art and design, graphics, music, English, drama, and modern languages. Periodically the individual programmes of study for the subjects within the curriculum area were suspended for a month and a topic such as advertising was selected as a theme for work throughout the curriculum area. Students wrote or analysed advertisements in English, designed promotional leaflets and booklets in art and design, devised and acted out their own 'television' advertisements in drama, with their own musical accompaniments, and examined foreign newspaper and television adverts in modern languages.

In science an integrated introductory course of physics, chemistry and biology is offered to the first two years. As with other subject areas, the course is being modified in the light of experience gained during the first year of teaching. The original basis was the Nuffield Science course, which some of the teaching staff had previously used elsewhere, but the staff have decided to develop their own schemes of work, lesson plans and worksheets to increase their flexibility in these initial years. The intention is to introduce the Suffolk Co-ordinated Science scheme in the third year, which leads to a double Mode 3 GCSE (Dobson 1989). Amongst the advantages seen in this course are that it is suitable for the whole ability range, that assessment is continuous, school based and genuinely criterion referenced, that it was developed by teachers, and that it has proved to be popular with girls as well as boys (O'Connor 1989).

Throughout the curriculum the CTC frequently uses textbooks which will be familiar to other teachers. In French the choice is *Escalier*, while personal and social education makes use of *Lifelines*. The *School Mathematics Project* (*SMP*) is used for mathematics teaching. By the second year, use of the Red and Blue tracks and the various extensions within *SMP* allows the teacher to juggle four levels of difficulty within the same mixed ability group.

The unfamiliar curriculum?

The introduction of business and economic awareness into the first year of the college is a major innovation. It is now common for

LEA schools to include such a subject in the later years, but it is still unusual for it to be included at age 11. Because of this, the course at the CTC is largely based upon materials developed for older children and produced by the Economics Association; it covers such topics as marketing, pricing, division of labour, and stocks and shares. One topic investigated during the time of the research was that of developing and selling a new portable radio. In small groups, students conducted market research on the preferences of students in other classes, and then developed and costed a simple 'ideal' product to match their results. Each of the four or five groups in the class then devised competing 'television' advertisements which they acted out in front of other students, who then voted for the product which they thought they would buy. In another long-running project, students were given shares in various companies whose fate they then followed through the stock market section of the major newspapers. It is recognized that none of these ideas is new in itself, and business and economic awareness has become an important part of the curriculum in many schools. Several aspects of the CTC course are often included elsewhere in the curriculum of pupils in many LEA schools. However, it is still unusual for such a course to be taught as a separate subject to 11–13 year olds.

In terms of the timetable, the three and a half hours given to enrichments is a far more important innovation than business and economic awareness. Enrichments is a name given to three time-tabled lessons where students are able to choose between a wide range of cultural and physical pursuits. There are two seventy-five-minute sessions on Wednesday afternoon, and a one-hour session on Friday morning. In part, enrichments incorporate within the longer CTC school day some of the activities which are regarded as voluntary extra-curricular activities in most LEA schools. Each term, students choose five options from a list of over forty, and practically all get three of their five choices. The range includes calligraphy, chess and computer programming, paper-making, pottery and photography, and squash, swimming and soccer. Students can make model aircraft, take part in the college dramatic production, guitar club or college band, or do weight-training, badminton or hockey. The list includes a wide range of sporting and other physical activities, and students must choose at least one, but not more than two, of this sort of enrichment, and have one or two 'non-physical' enrichments. Students who are learning a musical instrument are expected to take part in the college band or guitar club as appropriate. All options are open to all students, so the groups are mixed in age, gender and tutor group. Unlike several of the north Solihull LEA schools, the CTC does not have its own swimming pool, but makes use of the Solihull Swimming Pool which is just five minutes' walk away over playing fields. It also hires the adjacent Solihull Sports Centre to act as an extra sports hall during these enrichment times. The range of enrichments on offer is dependent upon staff interests, but is exceptionally wide as teaching staff appear to vie with each other to offer as diverse a list as possible and technical staff also teach some of the options. As might be expected, the enrichments are very popular with students.

Again the idea of having a wide range of negotiated enrichment activities is hardly without precedent in other schools. Various schools have set aside blocks of time in the week when pupils can choose from activities designed to enhance students' development outside the traditional academic curriculum. The options usually include sport, music, social or community work and various hobbies. Cowie and Rudduck (1988b: 38), for example, describe a case study school which first introduced such a scheme in 1983.

Within the private boarding schools the greater time available means that some form of option choice enrichment system is almost universal, and is aimed at widening students' experiences and views of the world (Walford 1986: 45). There is often a strong social service aspect to these activities in the public schools, which is not yet evident in the options available to the rather younger children at the CTC. In most LEA schools shortage of time acts as a pressure against including such enrichments within the school timetable. This pressure may well increase with the introduction of the National Curriculum, but at the CTC the longer school day enables them to be included as fixed and fully integrated lessons.

Teaching methods

The formal curriculum as defined by the timetable is only one aspect of the teaching and learning process that occurs within schools. The mode of delivery of the curriculum and the affective curriculum are also of major importance. The first two years of the

CTC curriculum are designed to be a preparation for the three-year GCSE courses that will follow, but they also have the major objective of building students' self-confidence and oral skills. Co-operative group work is a major feature of the teaching and learning strategy adopted in the college, and there is a far greater emphasis on oral work and presentation skills than is usual in schools.

The sponsors and governors of Kingshurst CTC have not been prescriptive in the curriculum for 11–16 year olds. There have been formal and informal meetings at which teachers and sponsors have discussed curriculum, but the sponsors have made no attempt to influence the details of the curriculum. However, sponsors do make clear their desire for young people who are able to take decisions, work with other people, write with reasonable accuracy, and talk intelligently and with confidence. It is to be hoped that these are aims of all schools, and following the Kingman Report (1988) on the teaching of English and the change to GCSEs there has been a growing emphasis on oral and communication skills in all schools. However, the CTC has made a point of emphasizing such objectives.

The ability to work with others and to take decisions is encouraged by the amount of co-operative group work that is used in all subjects. In music, for example, groups of four or five may be asked to develop their own improvised music to illustrate various moods or tell a story. Although there will be variation in musical ability, all students are expected to contribute ideas to the group. At the end of the lesson, the smaller groups present their music to the rest of the tutor group, after which it is discussed, praised and criticized. In PSE they may be asked to discuss bullying in groups and suggest why it occurs and how it could be stopped. Again, the groups are expected to organize themselves such that they can report back on their discussions to a plenary session. Sharing ideas is not regarded as 'cheating', but as good practice, and students are often asked to discuss possibilities for written work before starting to answer questions. In a similar way, in mathematics, students are encouraged to work together if they wish to do so, and it is recognized that students are often better able than teachers to unravel their peers' difficulties. The teacher's answer books are left out for students to decide for themselves whether they require the teacher's help.

Drama is another important area where group work is used to

encourage decision-making and creativity and to build self-confidence. The course starts by encouraging students to be observant of others around them. Students are set homeworks where they observe their parents watching television or working about the home. This individual work quickly gives way to sketches, where small groups are asked to improvise such scenes as 'chaos in the morning' or 'the burglary'. The enthusiasm is infectious, and after a couple of lessons students are frequently able to present impressively entertaining unscripted mini-dramas.

Self-confidence, creativity and the ability to work with others is also encouraged through one of the weekly assemblies, where each week a particular tutor group has responsibility for preparing and presenting an assembly for the whole college to last about fifteen minutes. Although the form tutor has final responsibility for ensuring that the presentation takes place, the content of these assemblies is very much a shared and negotiated responsibility with and between students. Most of these assemblies take the form of a series of mini-dramatic presentations in which all of the students from the form are involved. They are never dull.

I was with one second-year group during their day to present the assembly. They had chosen the theme of friendship – a topic which arose directly from their PSE work. They had spent two previous PSE lessons discussing what they wanted to do, gathering ideas, working in groups on mini-sketches, and making a video. They used an hour before the assembly to run through their presentation. It was constructed around the idea of a 'video friendship shop' where customers might choose new friends after viewing a video of them. Four students had prepared video advertisements of imaginary characters which were projected on to a large screen during the assembly. All of the characters presented were initially unpleasant and quickly rejected, which led the 'customers' to seek friends through more usual channels. Three short sketches followed involving four or five students each in which various aspects of being a good friend were acted out. In one case a supposed friend was talking unkindly about another behind her back, and was eventually found out. In another, a very popular boy, who had others grovelling at his feet for favours, was shown to be entirely self-centred, while in the third, the difficulties that a new pupil might have in making friends at school was shown. The customers returned to the video friendship shop still with no new friends, and viewed the rest of the four original videos in which more positive aspects of the characters were presented. The moral was drawn that we should take time to get to know people and not trust our first impressions.

The presentation was smooth, clear, well-structured and ambitious. The presenters brimmed with life and excitement and the audience responded enthusiastically. It involved all of the mixed ability group, and was genuinely entertaining. Anyone listening would have suspected that they had spent weeks learning a script and practising it. In fact there was no written script at all, and the mock performance I had viewed less than an hour before had differed considerably from the final version. By their second year at the college these students had sufficient self-confidence to be able to improvise dialogue within the framework that they had adopted for the sketches, and were able to respond appropriately to whatever the last person had said. They performed confidently in front of the whole school with only an occasional hiccup. Moreover, all of the student-led assemblies that I saw were of a similar high quality.

In observing classes involved in group work it was evident that the majority of students worked hard at the task for most of the time. Students frequently clearly enjoyed what they were doing. What was impressive in viewing lessons where group work occurred was the way in which students often helped less able members of the group, and were prepared to find aspects to praise in presentations which were not of the same standard as their own. Not all students worked equally hard, of course: a few students attempted to do as little as possible. However, such tactics made them undesirable future group members, as groups nearly always had to perform or report back to the whole class at the end. Occasionally a group's performance would make it clear that little work had been done, which they and other students found so embarrassing that it was unlikely to become a regular pattern.

The CTC Kingshurst is not alone in its stress on group work. The use of co-operative group work has increased greatly in many schools over the last decade or more, as an alternative means of organizing the classroom. Slavin (1987) has argued that under the right conditions the use of such co-operative learning methods increases student achievement, builds self-esteem and improves social relations among students. Of equal importance in the CTC context, co-operative group work is widely seen in a positive light by industry. While there is little consensus about what industry requires from schools in terms of curriculum content, there is greater agreement about the need for a flexible workforce which can work in teams and is capable of 'critical appraisal of process in the interests of the improvement of practice and ultimately of productivity' (Cowie and Rudduck 1988a: 9). Group work is widely accepted as fostering this aim and has been promoted by the Royal Society for the Arts (1983) through their Education for Capability programme, the Science and Technology Regional Organization (1987), within various TVEI schemes and by individual companies sponsoring educational change. For example, BP has sponsored a four-year project called *Learning Together, Working Together* based at the University of Sheffield (Cowie and Rudduck 1988a; 1988b). The seventy-eight local employers contacted in that study showed a high level of agreement on the importance of co-operative group work and its role in job satisfaction and efficiency.

Project Week

Another major innovation is Project Week, which in practice lasts about eight working days. Each term has a broad general theme to which individual teachers in part orientate their work. Past themes have included time, energy, and health and survival. The Project Week allows students to choose a group project on something related to the general topic which particularly interests them. The normal timetable is suspended for the period. Each tutor group is paired with another in the other year group, thus forming a mixed age group of about forty-seven students. The tutors for each of the groups and another teacher without regular tutorial responsibility are then given responsibility for the whole group for the period, giving a pupil/teacher ratio of about 16: 1.

The degree of freedom of choice that the students are given is to an extent dependent upon the teachers' style of working. Some teachers attempt to give the week an overall structure, and offer choices within that structure, while others are happy to let the groups choose to do a wide variety of only very broadly related topics. All students have to work in groups of about four to six. In some cases, students are free to choose whoever they wish to work with; in others, they are 'guided' by their teachers such that mixed age or mixed gender groups are formed. However, all of the groups are usually given considerable freedom to choose what they actually wish to do. They are encouraged to make their own decisions and know that at the end of the period they will be expected to present an impressive display board, or a model, machine, video, drama, game, musical production or similar.

One of the double tutor groups that I observed during their Health and Survival week spent their time working towards a production of a musical sonata called *Along Came Man*, which is concerned with the environment and the potential dangers of un-controlled technology. This group was amongst the most highly structured and teacher organized of the groups, and once about twenty-eight of the children had volunteered to take part, they were expected to work hard to produce a high-quality product. The sonata lasts about half an hour, and is not easy to sing. A major part of the week was thus spent in learning the music, which meant about two hours each day of intense concentration and hard work. But the students' week also had its easier moments where they worked on all the other aspects of putting on a finished perfor-mance. In smaller groups, some students designed and produced posters and programmes, others dealt with lighting, scenery, sound or special effects, others developed a dance sequence, or made costumes or papier mâché head-gear to represent extinct animals. The students enjoyed themselves, had plenty of time to chatter and discuss, but they also managed to achieve something worthwhile and entertain two groups of visitors with their final performances.

Students in most other double tutor groups spent their time working in smaller groups, with less overall structure. Some groups interpreted Health and Survival in terms of diet or fitness pro-grammes. They constructed questionnaires about diet and inter-viewed other students, sent away for information, or delved into books. Some went to a health centre to interview a dietitian, others visited a Safeway supermarket to see what people bought. During the week one large group visited the Museum of Mankind in Lon-don, and brought back ideas about constructing tents and surviving in harsh climates. Another large group used the week to think about survival away from the comforts of home, found information about tents, food, cold, and so on and finally camped out for a night.

About two-thirds of the way through the Project Week is a day when invited sponsors, industrialists, educationists and other important visitors are shown round the college by the college governors while work on the projects is in progress. Students are expected to be able to explain what they are doing to the visitors and to be able to answer questions. The Project Week ends with an open evening for parents and other guests at which practically all of the final results of the projects are on display. Students are again expected to be able to answer questions about their projects and explain what they have accomplished. At this event important visitors, who may be directors of sponsoring companies or of further companies that the college wants to woo, are shown round by students. The tour may last well over an hour, which is a heavy responsibility for a 12 year old to carry alone, but one which most appear to be able to discharge with confidence.

Understandably the effort put into projects varied from student to student. While some worked exceedingly hard, others exploited their freedom and did little during the week. Alongside some highly imaginative finished presentations of work, were others which were simply reproductions of passages taken directly from books. Such variation is inevitable, especially where there is a wide ability range. The teachers were faced with the difficult and exhausting problem of trying to balance freedom against structure. Where they saw potential problems they might ask a student to account for what he or she had done in the last hour, but they also had to be prepared to let children 'waste time', make mistakes and follow their own ideas. In general, students were not heavily monitored, but allowed to take their own decisions and be responsible for their consequences.

Project Weeks are not unique to the CTC. There are many other schools where the normal timetable is suspended for a period of days or weeks so that special activities can take place. One interesting example is Bishop McGregor School, which has been intensively studied by Robert Burgess since the 1960s (Burgess 1983; 1987), and had a similar project system for the first four years of its life. However, as the school grew in size, the complexity of organizing the event and increasing costs led to its abandonment. Of relevance to the particular status of the CTC, it is notable that several of the schools where this type of activity has occurred have been part of a broad progressive education movement, and have sometimes come into conflict with LEAs. Philip Toogood (1984), for example, who resigned his headship of Madeley Court Comprehensive in Telford, had regular weeks where teams of pupils worked on 'practical curriculum-led experiential learning'.

Post-16 curriculum

The CTC's proposal for the post-16 curriculum are distinctly different from the current curriculum of all LEA schools. It is widely recognized that GCE A level allows only a narrow and restrictive range of opportunities, which the introduction of AS levels has done little to improve. It also caters only for those young people of high ability who wish to study academic courses, probably leading to higher education. It is part of the CTC philosophy that education and training after 16 should be available to a far wider range of ability than this and that more young people should be encouraged to study for engineering, technology and vocationally orientated qualifications. The CTC has thus decided to make the Business and Technician Education Council's (BTEC) qualifications its major post-16 offering. At the time of writing (July 1990), the college had not yet admitted any post-16 students, so it is possible only to outline plans for the September 1990 intake. Changes may occur before that time, but they are unlikely to be major. The BTEC National courses planned include business and finance, engineering, science, computer studies, health studies, nursery nursing, travel and tourism, design technology, performing arts, leisure studies, and caring services. It is important to note that while some of these are specifically technologically based areas of study, others are not.

All of the above BTEC National Diploma courses last two years, and require at least three GCSEs graded C or above for entry. However, the college is taking seriously its remit to serve the whole ability range by also offering one-year BTEC First Diplomas to those students without this level of qualification. The college is to offer BTEC First Diplomas in business and finance, science, leisure studies, engineering, and caring, and many of these courses can be combined with Youth Training Schemes (YTS). The college would like the most successful of these students to be able to progress to BTEC National Diplomas, but is faced with the legal difficulty that CTCs are to cater only for 11–18 year olds, and the extra year's course would take some of the students over the 18-year-old limit. It is a further example of the problems generated by rapid and ill-thought-through legislation.

Alongside this variety of BTEC courses and the Kingshurst Diploma, which is an internal qualification that all students are intended to take, the CTC will offer the International

Baccalaureate (IB). A level courses will not be generally available, although students may be able to take an occasional A level if they wish. The International Baccalaureate has been adopted because it demands the study of a wide curriculum, and is the nearest existing publicly accepted university entrance examination to the Higginson proposals to reform A levels.

Over the last few years a range of international schools has developed to serve the children of mobile multi-national company executives, diplomats and others; the IB was originally created to provide these private international schools with a common curriculum at upper secondary level and a matriculation examination which had wide international acceptability. By 1989 there were more than 400 schools world-wide taking IB. Within the United Kingdom only about fourteen institutions are affiliated, including the United World College of the Atlantic, Sevenoaks School and several private sixth form colleges. The distinctive features of the course are that all students must study six subjects which span the social sciences, languages, natural sciences and mathematics. At least one foreign language is obligatory. All students also have to follow a theory of knowledge course, write an extended essay on some personal research and spend at least a half day each week on some form of creative aesthetic activity or active social service. It can be seen that the examination pattern has a number of congruences with the overall CTC philosophy of maintaining as broad a curriculum as possible for all. Although the IB is an entry examination for higher education, and usually available only to high-ability students, the CTC hopes to offer it to up to 50 per cent of its post-16 students. The belief is, quite simply, that children can achieve if they are given the encouragement and help to do so. It will be interesting to see the results after the first few years.

5

The students' view

Paula: It's not like a school, really. When you come through the gates, it's as if you're at home.

Zoe: Everyone's so friendly. And it's like, sort of, a community. Everyone's close. And I like all the technology and equipment. We do something different every day.

In the last few weeks before Christmas 1989 I individually interviewed forty-five of the second year students from three of the mixed ability tutor groups. These interviews were based on a questionnaire schedule derived from that used by Edwards, Fitz and Whitty (1989) in their study of the Assisted Places Scheme, but it was not rigidly adhered to and students were encouraged to talk as much as they wished. The areas covered included why they had chosen to go to the college, what they liked and disliked about it, their families, other interests and plans for the future. Each interview took about twenty minutes: most of the students quickly relaxed into the new situation, and were happy to agree to the interview being taped. I had the benefit of having sat for many hours in the same classes as they had. They knew that I already understood much about the college, and that whatever they said to me would not be passed on to teachers. All the names used here are pseudonyms.

Using the interview schedule and the students' answers as a framework, I also developed a written questionnaire which was given to six of the first year tutor groups and the other five second year tutor groups. In this case I took the whole class for a lesson by

myself, while they completed the questionnaires in a quiet atmosphere. All groups but one treated it very seriously, and it was
only one clique of boys in the last group which did not. Unfortunately a 'flu epidemic coincided with the last few weeks of term,
so the classes did not include all of the students. This made negotiating access with teachers far easier, but reduced the
coverage considerably. In all, 60 per cent of first year students
completed the questionnaire and 80 per cent of the second year
were either interviewed or gave written responses. As the questionnaire took about half an hour, with some groups I used the
extra time to have some class group discussions on their likes and
dislikes. In such a situation, peer pressure makes it difficult for
students to challenge the leading opinion, but it can produce some
valuable additional insights.

Interviewing children has its own problems, but the difficulty
of assessing their attitudes and opinions is not fundamentally different from that for adults (Walford 1991a). Both adults and children are influenced by people around them and by the interview
process itself, such that their answers are in part an echo of earlier
conversations. Many of the students had previously discussed their
reasons for choosing the CTC and their opinions about it with
other adults. For example, I was present during a class session when
one of the teachers asked the class to discuss with her what they
particularly liked about the CTC. Many had been asked such
questions by visitors to the college and by adults outside, and some
had even been interviewed by television reporters. The CTC students had thus thought about the issues before, and perhaps to a
greater extent than do similar children in other schools, but this
must be seen as a strength rather than a weakness. By considering
their motivations and opinions in class and elsewhere, they had
been able to clarify their thoughts. They were certainly not simply
parroting arguments.

Decisions and expectations

In interviews with the students I asked them to tell me about why
they had applied to the college, and whose choice it had been.
Inevitably many of them drew comparisons between the college
and their perceptions of other schools they might have attended.
Jonathan enthusiastically told me

Well, there isn't any other school that is as good as this, and I just wanted to see if I could get into it. When I read the booklet I really thought – this is my future – and I really wanted to come here and get a good job out of it.

Kevin replied that he had chosen to apply because

it was new and it had lots of technology in it, and I was told that I'd have a better chance with using new equipment. And you're supposed to have good prospects.

Other students voiced their reasoning in terms of 'a better education', 'a good chance in life', 'the best school for my education', 'because it was new', and so on. At this introductory stage of the interview most of the comparisons drawn were inexplicit, but some of the children named other schools that they would have attended and argued that the facilities there were poorer than available at the CTC. Unexpectedly several of the students also commented that they knew there was bullying at these other secondary schools, and being the first year through the CTC meant that there would be nobody older than themselves to bully them. For some of the students, this had been a major factor. Not all of this fear of bullying can be dismissed as 'transfer myths' (Measor and Woods 1984), for some of these children had brothers, sisters and friends who attended these other schools, who could tell them what happened there and who would also tell them about the facilities available in those schools.

To give a rough idea of how important the various factors were in the decision-making process, where possible, I classified the student's written comments into (1) those concerned with computing, technology and facilities of the college, (2) those linked to ideas of a 'good education' or 'better education', (3) those concerned with obtaining jobs or 'better' jobs and (4) those cases where what was important was that the college was new or different. There was, of course, overlap between the categories and students often gave more than one response. What was fascinating given the technological image of the CTC was that fewer than a quarter of responses were about computing, science, technology or related aspects. About one-tenth were concerned with the college being new or different, one-fifth expressed concerned with jobs and nearly half phrased their reasons in terms of a good or better education. (The variety of spellings for this word, including 'ejeekashon', 'egacation' and 'edgucason', testifies to the range of academic ability of the intake.) This idea of a better education might well include the computing and technological emphasis of the college, but it is interesting that so many students should express this in such a general way. In the interviews, I asked explicitly if it had been important to the students that it had been a *technology* college, and less than half claimed that it had been an important reason for their choice. As might be expected, there were those for whom computing had already been a hobby, who enthused about the chance to experience more powerful computers. In contrast, of those for whom technology had not been a major incentive, a typical reply was that given by Maurice, who said that it was 'Not really that important. I liked the idea. Technology was all right, but it was that it was a new school. Or Colin, who argued 'No, it was just that it was different from other schools that I wanted to come here. I never knew anything about computers before.' Or James who said, 'Well, it wasn't that important, I just thought that I might as well try and learn on the computers as well as the other stuff.' While technology may not have been a major reason for the choice, this does not mean that students were indifferent to it once they were in the CTC. At the time of the interviews, all three, Maurice, Colin and James highly valued the computing facilities.

Some of the students made it clear that it had been their parents who had made the decision to apply to the CTC rather than themselves. Some had been firmly against the idea at first, fearing that they would lose their friends or not be able to keep up with the work. Others, however, emphasized that it had been their own decision to apply. Helen told me:

> One of my friends said that she'd got a leaflet through the letter box. And she gave it to me and I read it, and she said I'd probably get one too. And when I got home there was one in the cupboard, and Mum was going to throw it away. She doesn't read things like that. So I said, 'Don't throw it away – read it, because it's about an application for a new school.' So she read it and we sent off.

The sad part of this story is that the friend also applied but was not accepted. Others of the students also told me that they had initiated the decision rather than their parents. Steven stated, 'Well, I told them about it first. They said "It's up to you. It's your career". They gave me the freedom what to do.' Joanna, too, 'Told my

Mum and Dad I wanted to go in for it and they said "It's up to you".' I was surprised the number of times I was told by students that they had first mentioned the CTC to their parents, rather than the other way round. Sean, who is very keen on computing, explained to me that his parents would have preferred him to try to go to King Edward's Grammar School, but he had refused to take the examination, arguing that he thought the CTC would be better with all the new technology it would have.

What students liked most about the CTC

All of the students interviewed or completing a questionnarie were asked what they liked and disliked about the CTC. The over-whelming majority of responses were very strongly positive, which was in accord with my experience of the students during the previous term. As is to be expected, students differed in the degree of their enthusiasm, but many of those interviewed bubbled into life as they told me about what they enjoyed about the place. So positive were many of the replies that it was often difficult for students to think of aspects of the CTC which they actually disliked, and it was only when asked how they thought the place could be improved that a few negative points emerged. I asked for positive points before negative ones, and only one of the students I interviewed avoided giving any positive points by answering directly with negative ones.

Students' responses do not sort themselves into straightforward categories. What they say about one area overlaps with other points. What Helen says below is a typical example of the comments from amongst the vast majority who were generally enthusiastic about the college.

Helen: I like all the computers and that. The lessons are good and there's lots of other things that are good – the teachers are good. Probably I've learnt more about computers and that than if I had been at other schools.

GW: What do you mean about the lessons being good?

Helen: Well, it's like, different. Like in the human studies lesson you can work on the computer or go to the typewriters and print it out, and you don't just have to sit down and write. Because you do more things.

GW: And the teachers are good too?

Helen: Yes, they're really good to you. Especially when I first came. They help you out, show you round. I just like the whole college. It's good, you know, most schools probably don't have social rooms and in a lot of them you have to go outside. But we get a choice. Most kids stay inside, except when you want to play football, then you go outside. You get the chance to be around college and watch television in break, and that.

GW: Why is that so important?

Helen: I don't like going outside, especially in winter. It's not so bad in summer. But inside, you can watch television and just sit around and talk to your friends before lessons. So it's more relaxed.

From Helen's comments, it can be seen that the aspects of the CTC that she appreciated overlap. However, many of the students focused their comments around (1) the technology and physical environment, (2) the friendliness of staff and other students, and (3) ideas of freedom and trust. These will be explored in turn from the students' viewpoints.

Technology and physical environment

As might be expected in a college which is designated a Technology College, the computers and other technology were important to many of the students. It has just been shown that some of the students had chosen to come to the CTC because they were already interested in computing, while others thought that it was important for them to understand computing and technology if they were to obtain good jobs. The level of attractiveness and comfort of the buildings was an additional benefit. Sarah, for example, told me, 'The equipment's really good, and I like the way you can use a computer in every lesson you're in. I like the way it's designed too. Different colours and that.' Alan told me that he liked

> All the computers. That you can use the computers at breaktime and you don't have to go outside. I like playing on the computers. I just like the style of the school. Like, the colours of it – the way it's all been set out. The furniture, too – it's comfortable.

I tried to find a quiet place for the interviews, and arranged two chairs at right angles to each other. I found that the recording studio was quite often free for this purpose. Several of the students would simply point at the video cameras and editing facilities in the room, would bounce a little on their comfortable chair, or point to the large potted plant in the corner. Why was I asking such obvious questions? Students would contrast what was available to them with what they believed pupils in other schools experienced. For example

James: The computers, I suppose. I went to [a nearby school] and they've got a few computers, but we've got them all round the place. It's comfortable – no wooden chairs – they're all padded. And there's a lot more resources.

Alister: People. I've made lots of friends. Technology. My brother's in the sixth form of [a nearby school] and he hasn't got half of what we've got. It's enjoyable to be here. Teachers are good.

Jason: Everything. It's like different. At my old school we had nothing like this. For the whole of the school – infants and juniors – we had five computers. That was quite a lot, but that's nothing to what we've got here. This is just very hi-tech.

These three examples, and various conversations I had with students, indicate that the availability of computers, while important, was not the only aspect of the technology and facilities that students appreciated. They welcomed an environment which was warm, comfortable and cheerful as opposed to what they perceived to be the cold uniformity and drabness of many schools. In their eyes several of the nearby schools were old, dull and in need of repair and redecoration. They complained of the graffiti they had seen on visits to other schools, of the hard chairs and worn-out desks. They believed that these other schools would not have as many video cameras, tape-recorders and the like, and they knew that there would not be a television and a video-recorder in every classroom.

Students were undoubtedly correct that the general quality of building, decoration and furnishing within the CTC was considerably higher than in other nearby schools. Critics of CTCs would argue that this is the direct result of high levels of funding from government and industry and that other schools could be equally attractive if the same amount of money were to be spent on them. Clearly there is much truth in this, but it is not the whole truth. One of the difficulties in drawing comparisons between the CTC and various LEA schools is that the CTC building and facilities have the clear advantage of being new and undamaged. Newness is in itself attractive, but much of Kingshurst's attractiveness comes not only from that newness but also from positive choices being made about the environment to be created. For example, it costs very little more to have a variety of colour schemes within a school, than it does to decorate all classrooms in exactly the same way. Yet most LEA schools are decorated in monotonously dull and unattractive colours. Again, it costs very little extra to have a variety of different furniture, rather than have 1,000 identical tables and chairs making each room look the same as the next, yet this is again what happens in most schools. In the same way, once the costs of cleaning have been taken into consideration, carpeting is not a luxury but a money-saver, and it costs very little more to have various colours than it would to have uniformity.

However, while something could be done to give all schools more pleasant surroundings with only minimal extra expenditure at the time of construction, an environment as good as that of the CTC could not be produced without some changes in priorities about school spending and additional funding. It was shown in Chapter 6 that Kingshurst's facilities are not uniformly excellent. A decision was made that artificial potted plants were initially more important to the CTC than a large library or multiple sets of science equipment. It may seem a slightly odd decision for a CTC to have made, but the evidence suggests that many of the students would agree with it.

Friendliness of staff and other students

In answering a question on what students liked most about being at the CTC, the friendliness of teachers and other students was referred to more often than computing, technology and facilities. They talked of the number of friends they had made, how the students were generally helpful to one another, and how they thought most of the teachers were approachable and interested in helping them. For example

Kirsty: I like the teachers because they're different from most other teachers. And it's different in the lessons, because we use more technology than most other schools do.

GW: What do you mean about the teachers being different?

Kirsty: They're kind. They're nice and kind to us.

Emma: Everything really. Because you can make friends really easily. Teachers are nice – they're friendly – all of them.

Tammie: Teachers. They're more friends than teachers. You can talk to them and have a joke and that. But as well as that you learn. I've learnt such a lot since I've been here. Every night I go home and tell my mum pieces of information that I've learnt.

GW: So your mum is learning a lot as well?

Tammie: Yes, and she's had to take up a night school class on computing to keep up with me!

Catherine gave a more considered, and perhaps more accurate view, of the friendliness of the CTC:

And there's a friendly atmosphere too – the friendly atmosphere can have its on and off days – but it's usually quite friendly. Staff are really good. You can talk to all of them as if they were one of your friends, which is good. Yet they can be strict when they're meant to be. And they can be soft and they can have a laugh with you too. When it's called for to have a laugh, then they'll have a laugh with us, but they won't take it too far either, which is another good thing. They'll stop before it gets out of hand.

Not all the students felt quite this positive about the teaching staff, and very few made specific comments against named teachers when talking about what they disliked about the college, but the overall feeling was very positive, and this was evident from classroom observation. The college does have an informal, yet structured, atmosphere, and teachers do take time to talk and listen to students in non-teaching time as well as in lessons. The slightly more generous staffing ratio is one factor which make this more possible, but probably more important is the selection of staff, and the enthusiasm which is generated by being part of something new. It was shown in Chapter 4 that the college tries to foster co-operation and uses group work extensively in teaching. It also tries to build student's self-esteem and confidence, all of which can be done only in an atmosphere of mutual respect between teachers and students. That students perceive the college as a friendly place must be seen, at least in part, as a sign that the college is achieving success in this area.

This interpretation is not unchallengeable, however, as Edwards *et al.* (1989: 200) obtained similar expressions about the friendliness of their particular school from pupils in many of the private and state-maintained schools where they conducted their Assisted Places research. They quote children as saying that their school has a 'friendly' or 'homely' atmosphere, and one girl who states that 'it just doesn't feel like a school', which is remarkably similar to Paula's comment at the start of this chapter. The difference, however, is that most of the pupils interviewed by Edwards *et al.* were of high academic ability, while the CTC students spanned the ability range, and the extent of these comments at the CTC would appear to be greater than in their schools. Nevertheless, Edwards *et al.*'s findings do indicate that children's views about their own school must be treated with some care. Most of them have only their primary schools to draw comparisons with, and few in the CTC sample had very much positive to say about that experience.

Another unexpected aspect of the friendliness expressed by many of the students was the lack of bullying at the CTC. It was shown earlier that thoughts about possible bullying at other schools had influenced a number of the students to apply to the CTC. Bullying was often mentioned by students, particularly by the girls, when asked how they thought the CTC differed from the school they would otherwise have gone to. For example Joanna, who had visited the school in question, said:

> It's like, all the older people they bully you. Here we're the oldest so we can boss all the younger ones round (laugh). There's no bullying at this school. Nothing like that.

Moreover, it was not just one other school where it was thought that bullying occurred, but most of them. Claire told me, 'At [another school] they've got all bullies and things, and there's not here, because they're all friendly.' Chantal claimed that 'at [another school] a lot of bullying goes on.'

The children's perceptions about bullying were not entirely

correct. It was undoubtedly correct that some bullying occurs in other local schools, but it was not true that it was entirely absent from the CTC. I saw a few minor cases during my term at the CTC, but this was far less than I would expect elsewhere, and the few cases were against particular children who would probably have fared far worse elsewhere. Bullying was certainly not a problem at the CTC but, of course, in 1989 there were only two age groups at the college, with none over 13. What is significant is that students picked this out as one of the aspects which they valued.

Ideas of freedom and trust

The third group of aspects which students said they liked about the college present something of a conundrum. Many of the students I interviewed and who wrote about the CTC said that they liked the freedom of the place. To an independent observer, the concept of freedom does not mesh very closely with the highly structured and largely teacher-controlled environment of most schools. For the most part, children at school are told what to do and when to do it. Their lives are regulated by the whims of the particular adults put in charge of them. Chapters 3 and 4 have shown that Kingshurst was not a modern-day equivalent of the 1960s free schools, where children were able to choose whatever they wanted to do. What, then, were the aspects of the CTC which students interpreted as freedom? As some students tried to explain, they centred on two features. The first is the degree of flexibility allowed to students within lessons.

Kevin: You're allowed more freedom. In lessons you're allowed to go out – they don't chain you to a desk like some other schools do.

Jonathan: And we're free – we can go out in lessons, type things up and everything.

Steven: You get a lot of freedom and the teachers encourage you. At our old school they never even told us what to do, they just said 'get on with it'.

GW: What do you mean by freedom?

Steven: Well, it's like, they give you what you can do and you get on with it, and if you need help come and get it. They say, go away and do whatever *you* want about whatever you're doing.

Lessons differed according to teacher, subject and particular aspect of the curriculum being studied in each lesson. In some cases students might just as well have been 'chained to the desks' for they did not move from their seats for the whole hour. But students were correct in implying that this was not the general rule. In music, for example, students might do desk work for a while, but would also work in groups developing their own music or sing together as a class group. In science or food technology the perceived tedium of written work would be alleviated by practical work on video tape-recordings. In human sciences, students might be working together on projects, and could be using word processors or electronic typewriters as well as pen and paper.

In the quote above, Steven is trying to explain how, in subjects such as art and design and craft, design and technology, students were encouraged to think for themselves and not just follow given instructions. For example while I was there students were given what the teacher called a 'boring task' of making a folder to keep their future work in. They were instructed to make the task more interesting by being imaginative, and by using whatever facilities they wished. Thus while some students used traditional paints or made collages, others went off to take photographs to use on the folder, others worked in fabrics, or carved clay from which thin plastic vacuum mouldings were later taken. The finished folders were each individual personal creations, and students had been encouraged to take their own decisions during the making process rather than rely on teachers' ideas. It was not just that they were free to move physically from one working area to another – often in different parts of the building – but that they were free to make their own decisions and mistakes about their own work.

This freedom was also sometimes evident in lessons which might be traditionally desk bound. English might include mini-dramas, or work involving word processing or display. As computers were scattered around the college, word processing could mean not only leaving the classroom, but also finding an unused computer elsewhere and working in the midst of another class's lesson. Students from one class group would frequently be found working on computers in a classroom where a completely different lesson was in progress. Mathematics might mean a walk to the playing field to measure it with pedometers. Little of this, of course, is unique to Kingshurst, but the atmosphere was such that teacher-led desk work was perceived to be only a part of what teaching and learning was about. Students were given freedom to make choices within much of what they did.

The concept of freedom also had a specific association within the CTC, as Edmund explains:

Edmund: There's more freedom. My old school, during breaks we were made to go outside, stay outside even in the rain. And then come inside after. We weren't trusted at all at my old school. There were a few bad characters there, but most of us were all right, and they just didn't trust anyone.

Mark: The freedom. What you're allowed to do. You can just come in at dinner-time and sit down. In my old school you weren't allowed in the building at dinner-time or break-times, because the equipment got broken, but here they're trying to get it so you don't break anything. So everyone tries to be sensible.

Lee: At other schools, you just wouldn't be able to do anything at break. You'd get chucked out. You can do anything here. Computers are good, too. There's a lot of games, and there's different things you can learn each day. So you learn as well as having fun.

Again and again students made it clear to me just how much they valued the very simple freedom of being allowed to stay inside the college buildings during break-times. They could use the computers to play games, watch television, sit and talk, or sometimes rush wildly round the college until someone stopped them. In fact, they were allowed to do the sorts of things in the college that they would do in their own homes, which meant that the 'simple' freedom of being allowed to remain in the buildings altered the students' relationship with the college in some fundamental ways. While students recognized that their rights were conditional upon appropriate behaviour, they treated the college as if it were their own property as much as the teacher's. They said they were and seemed to be 'at home' in the classrooms, for they were places where they socialized with friends. They knew that some offices were private, but they had little hesitation in using designated equipment spread throughout the college. Life was not always harmonious. For example shortage of computers meant that some students were verbally bullied away from them, but few would have replaced this sometimes abused freedom by close teacher control. Learning to sort out problems is a vital lesson.

What students disliked about the CTC

The overwhelming message from students was that they enjoyed being at Kingshurst but, inevitably, there were some aspects which did not meet with approval. Students interviewed and who answered questionnaires were asked what they disliked about the CTC as well as what they most liked: 31 per cent of the first year and 11 per cent of the second year students either left this question blank (about a third) or stated positively that there was nothing they disliked. The strength of some of these feelings can be gauged by the severity of the comments: 'absolutely nothing', 'nothing at all' and similar.

Of those who did have complaints, most wrote or spoke about only a single item. Fewer than 20 per cent mentioned more than one problem area. About 10 per cent of each year complained about specific lessons or teachers, usually in terms of simply not liking the subject, or of particular problems with certain teachers. There were no detectable patterns in the lessons mentioned. The overwhelming number of negative responses were concerned with just two areas – homework and college hours. In the first year 13 per cent of the students complained about the homework, but this rose to 30 per cent for the second year. The complaints were in terms of there being too much homework and of the homework being too difficult. Students took trouble to explain the CTC system of three homeworks each night of about thirty minutes, and would sometimes compare that with what they knew pupils at other nearby schools were expected to do. Some even explained that, although they did not like doing that amount of homework, they believed that it would be 'good for them' in the end, particularly in terms of getting 'a better job'. An argument used several times was that the amount of work set was especially unfair considering the long hours that they worked at college and, indeed, the major pairing of dislikes was between the amount of homework and the length of the college day.

College hours obtained more negative comments than any

other item: 30 per cent of the first year and 38 per cent of the second year stated that they disliked the hours. This was sometimes expressed as a dislike of the length of the college day as such, and sometimes as a distaste for the early start time. In both cases, however, the implication was practically always that a shorter day was desirable. The two following written answers to the question about dislikes are typical of responses of this sort:

87: The only thing I don't like is having to get up at 7.00 in the morning. The hours we go and leave school is horrible. Also loads of homework.

82: The time we have to come to school in the morning. I don't think I'll ever get used to getting up so early. Also the amount of homework, it gets too much at times.

Some students showed the strength of their feelings by choosing words such as 'detest' or 'hate' to describe the early start to the day. Others made it clear that they felt they had good reason for such feelings – they became tired by the end of the day, they had to travel to and from college in the dark, it was almost like office hours, or that the long day plus the homework meant that they had little time for any other outside activities.

The exact figures for dislike of the college's hours are a little open to question for the questionnaire also contained a specific question which asked 'What do you think about the longer school day here?' However, this second question was placed later in the questionnaire and none of the students wrote about their dislikes using the phrase 'longer school day'. This second question brought out many more replies (including several from those who had previously stated that they had no dislikes) which indicated that the majority of students did not favour the early start and the late end to the day. Tiredness and lack of time for other activities once the homework was done were common claims. Some were just resigned to it, for example:

27: I don't think there is any need for the longer school day, but now we've got it there is nothing we can do about it, so I suppose it's all right.

31: I think it's all right, but it doesn't leave you much time. You work all day and when you get home you have homework to do, in between this I stop for my tea. By the time I've finished my homework, it is time for bed.

164: I don't really like it but I learn more in school.

In contrast, a sizeable minority saw the longer day in a positive light. They enjoyed being there, so a longer day was good. It gave more time for lessons, so they would learn more. It kept them busy when they would only be wasting time at home. Others claimed that, as the hours just flew by, they didn't even notice. This seemed to be literally true for one student who claimed, 'We don't have longer days!' In all, though, the evidence was that the longer school day, which was a feature of the description of the CTCs in the original DES (1986) document but was not explicitly included in the 1988 Education Reform Act, was not popular amongst students. Perhaps more importantly, although many students claimed that they got used to the longer hours, stronger negative feelings were expressed by the second year than the first year. If the trend were to continue, this could become a major problem for the college in the future.

Finally, it is worth considering the range of other negative points which some students reported. About 30 per cent of student dislikes could not be classified under the categories so far discussed. The range was wide. About 3 per cent of each year complained about the college having three floors and that it was tiring for them to climb the stairs. A further 4 per cent argued that the college was too small and the corridors too cramped. About the same number disliked the uniform, and another small group disliked queues for meals. The rest of the areas of dislike had only one or two endorsements. For example, two students stated that they disliked their own class, one hated the building site, two found the number of visitors to the college unpleasant, one specifically wanted to be able to chew gum in the college, while another thought it unfair that teachers could eat elsewhere in the college while they could do so only in the dining-hall. Finally, two brave souls stated that they disliked the computers!

6

The selection process

Nigel: Well I didn't really choose it. My mum and dad said, 'Would you like to go to this school?' and I didn't really know much about it. They said it was a new school, and I said I'd have a go trying to get in, and if I didn't go there I'd go to Simon Digby. And the test was sorting things out, seeing what shapes fitted with other shapes. So that was fairly easy, and they took people over the ability. So they have some with high ability and some with low.

GW: And where do you think you are?

Nigel: About the middle. And the interview was quite interesting. I can't remember who I had – someone who wore glasses, don't see him very often, he comes in now and again – and we had to take something we were interested in. I took in a model airplane. Can't remember the name of it now. And he asked me questions about it. What engines does it use, and did I know? He asked me to spell certain words, talked to my parents, asked me about calculators and just generally talked about the school.

The original DES booklet outlining the CTC scheme made it clear that CTCs

will not be neighbourhood schools taking all comers; nor will they be expected to admit children from outside the catchment area. Their admission procedures and catchment areas

will need to be defined in such a way as to give scope for
selecting pupils from a number of applicants. The precise
arrangements will need to be decided case-by-case but a typical catchment area is likely to contain at least 5,000 pupils of
secondary age, from whom 750–1,000 pupils will be
admitted.

(DES 1986: 5)

As discussed in Chapter 3, it was this emphasis on selection of
children, and its implied attack on the comprehensive system,
which has been at the heart of the continued controversy sur-
rounding the City Technology Colleges. This chapter examines
the selection procedures adopted by Kingshurst CTC and the
effects of that selecting process on the children themselves and on
nearby local authority schools. It is worth stressing again that all of
the CTCs are separate independent schools and what is done at
Kingshurst may be different from what is done elsewhere,. The
college itself may also gradually change some of the details of its
selection procedure.

Catchment areas

In Chapter 2 it was shown that the site for this first CTC was
carefully chosen such that a catchment area could be drawn which
would include homes in east Birmingham as well as in north
Solihull. As explained in Chapter 2, although not an inner-city
area, it is predominantly a characteristic Labour-voting working-
class area, composed almost entirely of Birmingham overspill
council built estates. The map given in Chapter 2 (see p.22)
showed that the catchment area used for the first year's intake in
September 1988 was a rather unusual shape. The site of the CTC
itself is some way off-centre from a broadly circular boundary with
a diameter of about four miles, which encompasses a slightly larger
area of Birmingham than of Solihull. However, it is important to
note that two irregular 'bites' were taken from the circle. To the
north, a wedge of housing trapped between the M6 motorway and
the A47 Chester Road is excluded from the catchment area even
though it is within Solihull, while to the south, an area in Birmingham north of the A45 Coventry Road and near to the International Airport has also been omitted. Both of these areas – Castle

Bromwich and Sheldon – include a higher proportion of middle-class families living in privately built housing, and were excluded when the catchment area was first negotiated in 1987.

The catchment area was altered in two ways for the 1989 and subsequent intakes. First, it was decided that 5 per cent of the intake could be taken from outside the catchment area and, second, the catchment area itself was enlarged to include Castle Bromwich and part of Sheldon. The Principal argued that both of these changes were made to give the college a more comprehensive intake in terms of social class and ethnic mix, and to reduce the number of problems with parents living on the 'wrong side of the road' forming the boundary. As the original catchment area is almost entirely white with a few Afro-Caribbean families, there had been no Asian children in the first year's intake, and only a very small number of Afro-Caribbean. The 5 per cent taken from outside the catchment area (nine children each year) enables a better ethnic mix of children to be achieved in the college. This is certainly the way in which it was used for the 1989 intake with four or five of the nine selected from outside being of ethnic minority backgrounds.

It is worth noting, however, that the college does not pay transport costs for these students, so there is a financial disincentive for many outside the catchment area to apply. The college also does not make any strong attempt to attract students from outside the catchment area, and does not distribute information leaflets to homes outside the boundary. This is a logical limitation, given the very small number of places available to those not living within the catchment area, but it means that those who apply have to be amongst those already highly informed about local educational provision.

Valerie Bragg uses similar arguments about increasing the comprehensiveness of the intake to explain the changes made to the catchment area itself, as she sees it as good for the college as a whole to have just a few more children from professional backgrounds. She argues that a comprehensive school benefits from having some middle-class children who can help raise the aspirations of other children at the college. Judging from the primary schools of the sample of children in the first year who completed questionnaires, it would seem that about 5 per cent of the intake have benefited from this boundary change. The college has thus not drawn disproportionately from these newly included areas.

There may have been an additional unvoiced reason for the catchment area change. Although there had been nearly 1,000 enquiries about entry for the first intake, fewer than 400 had actually applied and only about 360 of these were valid applications for children of the correct age and living within the original catchment area. This number is not particularly high when 180 places are on offer. From the out-catchment applications and many other enquiries, it was known that a demand existed outside, which would give the CTC a little more choice in selecting a range of children.

It is important to see these catchment area changes in the context of changes in national policy towards the CTCs. The original catchment area and the later changes had to be agreed by Kenneth Baker. The line had originally been established by the college and some of its original advisers at a time (mid-1987) when the rhetoric was still that the CTCs were to serve only disadvantaged inner-city children. It was drawn very tightly to exclude areas where there might be any doubt about the social class composition of the residents. By mid-1988 it had become evident that other CTCs would be taking a far less rigid definition of their potential clientele than had Kingshurst, and it was possible to include the two irregular 'bites' in the circle. The changes to the catchment area and the inclusion of a few children from outside the area might also be seen as being congruent with ideas of magnet status for the CTCs. In the USA magnet schools were associated with increased social class and ethnic group mixing. However, these modifications to eligibility were relatively minor and the catchment areas of some other CTCs are far wider than the revised Kingshurst catchment area. Again, while the DES booklet (DES 1986: 5) stated clearly that CTCs would not be expected to admit children from outside the catchment area, by the time the Education Reform Bill was published in November 1987 the pupils were to be 'wholly or mainly drawn from the area in which the school is situated' (Clause 80 (2) (b)). It is an example of how the gradual changes in policy at the national level affected this first CTC and, perhaps, vice versa.

At post-16 level, the catchment area is far wider and extends to the whole of Solihull, Birmingham and part of Warwickshire. In the first three years it is expected that students will be drawn from a wide diversity of schools, but after that the majority of students will come from the lower part of the college. The college hopes that post-16 education will be provided for about 500 students both from inside the CTC and from other schools.

Selection process

The college's special status, independent of any local education authority, has major implications for the selection procedure adopted. It is treated by the Education Departments of both Birmingham and Solihull in exactly the same way as other independent schools, in that it is simply not mentioned in any information sent to parents about admission arrangements to secondary schooling and no effort is made by the Education Departments to encourage children or parents to apply.

In Solihull, secondary school applications are conducted on an inertia principle. A booklet is made available for parents which gives details of all LEA and voluntary secondary schools in the borough, but children are allocated to a particular secondary school on the basis of catchment areas (unless they attend a Roman Catholic Aided primary school where they are allocated to one of the two Roman Catholic secondary schools). Parents are told how they can express a preference for a school other than that allocated, but it is assumed that those who make no contact are happy with their allocated schools. As explained in Chapter 2, Birmingham still retains a selective system. Parents have to apply for their child to take an entrance examination for one of the grammar schools and, each year, about half of those children eligible take the test. About 9 per cent of the total cohort are selected, it being more difficult for a girl to gain a place than a boy. Those not selected are given a place at one of the county or voluntary 'comprehensive' schools. Until 1990, parents of all children due to transfer to secondary schooling (which takes place at 11 for most of the borough, but at 12 for the Sutton Coldfield district) were sent a large (A4) booklet with about a page of information on every school in the borough. Parents are asked to list three schools in order of preference. Allocation to schools is made centrally by the Education Department on the basis of publicly advertised criteria which take account of special educational needs, the distance of the home from the school, the presence of a sibling already at a school and the parents' preference order of schools. In 1989 91 per cent of pupils were given their first preference school, and 97 per cent received one of their three preferences. At the official level, neither Birmingham or Solihull provide parents with any information about the CTC. In practice, some teachers and headteachers of primary schools in both boroughs are prepared to give advice.

As information about the CTC is not given to parents of 10 year old children by the LEAs, and as neither LEA provides the CTC with a list of such parents, the CTC has to advertise widely each year to attract each new entry. The details have varied slightly over the three years of operation, but the following stages have been followed. A simple full-colour leaflet is delivered to all 50,000 or so homes in the catchment area. It stresses that Kingshurst is the first of the CTCs, that it offers a new choice for parents, and that it is free. A brief description of the curriculum is given, along with information on outdoor activities, enrichments, the hi-tech equipment and links to the community, industry and commerce. There are colour photographs of students outside the college and at work inside the classrooms. A post-free postcard is enclosed which parents return for an application form and further information. For the first year's intake parents received a simple but attractive eight-page A5 booklet and an application form, but since then a more expensive A4 folder has been used which contains several sheets of thin card with further information and colour photographs printed on one side only. A feature of the booklet is an attached fold-down page which carries about twenty highly positive comments on the college from named CTC students. The folder and contents are impressively designed, although rather shorter on factual content than some of the prospectuses of nearby LEA schools.

Every child who has an application form returned is offered an interview. There were about 360 valid applications in the first year, about 550 in the second and about 730 in the third. The applicants are interviewed with at least one adult for about thirty minutes. This is usually the child's parents, but sometimes it has been a grandparent or another relation. Valerie Bragg has publicly told the story of one child who brought along a grandfather in the hope that 'he would be all right', because his parents 'did not want to come'. Children bring something with them to talk about – a toy, something they are proud of, something they have made – to try to put them at their ease and to act as an initial focus for discussion. The meeting is also used to talk with parents, to tell them about the longer day, the level of work expected and the commitment to staying in full-time education until 18. An attempt is made to indicate that there is a bias towards practical work, project work and group work and that the CTC was not a school where the children were sitting at desks and writing all the time. It is recognized that some children might be better suited to a more traditionally structured regime, and a few parents are counselled accordingly.

Children are also called to the college in groups to complete a simple standardized National Foundation for Educational Research non-verbal test, which takes about thirty minutes of writing time. The three raw scores from the different parts of the test are added together and a single standard age score calculated which takes into account the age of the child on taking the test. These standard age scores are then compared with the national sta*nines* which divide the distribution of scores into *nine* parts. Nationally about 20 per cent of scores will have a stanine value of 5, which includes all those results which are within 0.25 standard deviations of the mean. Stanine 6 runs from 0.25 to 0.75 standard deviations above the mean and contains about 17 per cent of the distribution, and so on. The extreme stanines of 1 and 9 include all those scores of greater or less than 1.75 standard deviations from the mean respectively – about 4 per cent in each case. The college calculates a normal distribution for all those taking its test and finds the appropriate quota to be taken from each stanine. The vast majority are taken from stanines 4, 5 and 6.

Selection of individuals within each stanine is based upon information available from the interviews and from the Heads of the primary schools, who are all asked to provide a reference. In the first year, further controversy was caused by the simplicity of the report form sent to primary schools, which asked the Head to underline as appropriate whether the child's ability was 'well above average', 'about average' or 'well below average' and to assess the child's suitability for the CTC in a similar three-fold division. This form is no longer used, and has been replaced by one which asks for a classification of 'excellent', 'good', 'satisfactory' or 'poor' for each of eight factors. These eight include academic ability, effort shown, practical skills, thought/imagination, behaviour, health, attendance and social skills. There is also a space for Heads to make further general comments. However, as Birmingham LEA has a policy of non-cooperation with the CTC, some Heads reply to requests for information while others do not. Inevitably this may put some children at a disadvantage, for within each stanine the

CTC is looking for the most suitable children, and there is bound to be a tendency to take those children with positive references rather than those with no reference at all. The differences in the degree to which Heads co-operate with the CTC is also reflected in the number of applications received from each school. While some Heads will actively encourage children to apply, others will avoid any mention of the CTC to parents. This led to some bunching of applications in the first year's intake, with one primary school providing fourteen of the accepted students. However, for both years, students have been drawn from more than forty different primary schools. This bunching is less for the second intake, but a greater number of students is likely to be accepted from schools where there are more applicants.

The area covered by the catchment within Birmingham is larger than that in north Solihull but it was still originally intentioned that roughly equal numbers of children should be drawn from each part. In the first year of operation there were 180 valid applications from north Solihull and 122 from Birmingham, which led to slightly more children from Solihull than from Birmingham being selected. Roughly equal numbers of children from each area were selected for the second intake year. For the third year of operation there were about 730 applicants who took the test, with more from Birmingham than Solihull.

The interviews with applicants are conducted by the Principal, the Director of Finance and Administration, the Industrial and Commercial Liaison Officer, and the Area Managers. For the first intake, at a time when there were few staff appointed, some retired Headteachers were also involved. In selecting students, the college's first criterion is that those selected have a range of academic abilities and are representative of those applying in terms of these stanines. However, the college also has a clear policy with regard to gender and ethnic mix. It aims to take an equal number of boys and girls and have an ethnic mix with at least as many ethnic minority students as in the area. Other criteria are more difficult to specify explicitly. The rather more elusive abilities to enthuse, to chat, to have something to offer, are the sorts of attributes that interviewers are looking for, but there are no rigid criteria. Students do not have to have competence in computing or technology to be accepted. The final decision as to which students are accepted is made by the Principal.

Some results of selection

It is important to investigate the characteristics of the students selected by the process outlined above, and to discuss the likely effects of selection on these students. This section will consider questions of IQ distribution, social class distribution and the extent to which these children and their parents might be considered to be already able to exploit the educational system to their own advantage.

IQ distribution

When the first intake of students was announced there was considerable debate about whether the CTC had selected fairly. The average IQ score for north Solihull was stated to be around 90, whereas that for the children admitted was 98. The average for the second intake was 96.4, even though the catchment area has been increased. The difference between the north Solihull score and the average for the CTC might be accounted for, in part, by the average IQ for the east Birmingham area being higher than that for north Solihull. However, in practice, the college's decision to select students to be representative of those who apply is the crucial decision. The method of choosing within stanines could also lead to a higher average IQ for those selected than for those applying, simply because individuals at the top of each stanine could be chosen. However, technically, even the original DES booklet did not state that the intake had to be 'representative' of the ability range in the catchment area, but only that the colleges 'should aim at admitting pupils spanning the full range of abilities represented in the catchment area' (DES 1986: 5). The 1988 Education Reform Act reduced this to the far more modest duty to provide education for 'pupils of different abilities' (105 (2) (b)), so the college is going way beyond what is legally required in attempting to be representative of those who apply. The college has two children who are statemented as having special educational needs, and several more who might benefit from such statementing.

Social class distribution

A number of commentators in CTCs (see for example Morrell 1989; Simon 1988; Walford 1990a; 1990b) have suggested that selection by interview and recommendation from primary school Heads could easily lead to a disproportionate number of middle-class children being accepted. It has been argued that middle-class children are more likely to be able to present themselves well at interview and behave more acceptably in primary school, which would lead to their being accepted in disproportionate numbers. Thus even if the spread of abilities, as measured by IQ tests, is representative of the catchment area (or of those within the area who apply), it is suggested that middle-class parents are more likely to apply on behalf of their children and their children are also more likely to be accepted.

The results from the individual interviews and questionnaires from students at Kingshurst enable some insight to be gained on these predictions. In both cases students were asked 'What do your mother and father do?' In the interviews, this question was probed as carefully but as sensitively as possible, while the questionnaires encouraged students to 'Please give as much detail as you can'. The questionnaires were answered individually by students in class groups. This meant that the students did not all complete the questionnaires at the same time, and wanted to hand them to me once they had written as much as they wished. In many cases this gave me the chance to ask gently for a few more details on parental occupations if what they had written was unclear or insufficiently detailed. I was unable to check every case, but I did manage to look at more than half of the answers on parents' occupations and to ask for further clarification where necessary.

Asking 11–13 year old children about their parents' jobs has several difficulties. The most obvious one is that they simply may not know exactly what their parents do. They may know where they work, but not what sort of job they actually perform. In their study of the Assisted Places Scheme Edwards *et al.* (1989: 161) found that children were often vague and 'over-optimistic' about the work that their parents did. This could be due to lack of knowledge, parents giving their children a false impression or due to children wishing to give the interviewer a good impression. It is likely that similar 'over-optimism' occurred here, with the additional difficulty that these children cover a far wider ability range than the children interviewed by Edwards *et al*. However, these authors also found that the distribution of parents' occupations as described by their sample of children was broadly similar to the distribution obtained by interviewing those parents directly. We must not expect a perfect correlation between what students say their parents do and what they actually do, but the distribution of jobs is worth considering.

In interviewing the students at Kingshurst CTC, it quickly became evident to me that it would be sensitive to ask first whether they still lived with their mother and father before asking about their parents' jobs. This enabled a large number of students to explain their own particular circumstances if they wished to. I have taken the terms 'mother' and 'father' to indicate the adults within the household who have a continuing relationship with the child. In some cases this is a stepfather, or occasionally a partner with no legal responsibility for the child, but where the child regards that person as a father. For simplicity, the question was phrased only in terms of mother and father on the questionnaires, but some students explained the relationship between them and the person whom they regarded as mother or father. I told students that they need not answer any question if they did not want to. Within the second year two students omitted to answer this question for both their parents. A few other answers were too vague to be classified, and several of the students gave only one parent's occupation, usually because it was a single-parent household, but this may sometimes have been because the mother was not in paid employment.

The college does not keep records of the identities of adults who share the household with the student and guardian. Obviously it records the names and addresses of legal guardians, but it does not necessarily know the marital status of the guardian, or with whom the guardian is cohabiting. It would have been inappropriate to have asked students about this, so it is not possible to give an accurate indication of the proportion of students in single-parent families. The Principal has estimated that about half of the students are no longer living with both natural parents, and the information gained through interviews does not contradict this estimate.

In view of the uncertainties with parents' occupations, it is not appropriate to use a highly detailed or sophisticated system of social or socio-economic classification. I have thus used the social class classification used by the Office of Population Censuses and

Surveys in their ten-yearly censuses as used in Chapter 2. Here, the unit groups within the occupational classification are gathered together into broad categories from I to V. Social class I refers to professional and other similar occupations, II to intermediate occupations, and III to the skilled occupations, divided into N (non-manual) and M (manual). Social class IV refers to the partly skilled and V to the unskilled occupations. Table 6.1 shows the distribution of occupations separately for men and women nominated as father and mother by the students who were selected for the first year of operation of the college.

Table 6.1 gives the percentage of adults in each category according to the descriptions given by the students; 80 per cent of this year were either interviewed or answered questionnaires. No attempt has been made to establish whether any of the 16 per cent of women who were seen to be houseworkers perceived themselves as unemployed, or whether any of the 7 per cent classified as unemployed perceived themselves as houseworkers. None of the students classified their unemployed fathers as houseworkers.

The most clearly evident aspect of the figures displayed in Table 6.1 is the low percentage of parents in professional or similar occupations. Without putting too much faith in the exact numbers, it is evident that only a very small percentage of adults are from social class I, and that not very many more are from either class I or II together. The vast majority of adults have skilled manual or non-manual occupations. The women are typically secretaries, clerical workers or shop assistants, while the men are in various types of engineering, or may be tool-makers, bus drivers or electricians. From social classes IV and V are to be found a fair number of labourers, factory workers, kitchen hands and cleaners. The exact figures are open to doubt but, especially when it is remembered that children probably have a tendency to over-

Table 6.1 Social class of parents of first intake year students (percentages)

	I	II	IIIN	IIIM	IV	V	Unemp.	House-worker	Student
Men N = 119	1	9	12	49	21	2	6	0	1
Women N = 120	0	9	45	4	16	3	7	16	0

estimate their parents' jobs, it is certain that this first intake year at Kingshurst does not include a high proportion of middle-class children as many commentators had predicted.

The uncertainties with students' level of understanding of their parents' jobs is greater with 11–12 year olds than with 12–13 year olds. Questionnaires were completed by a random sample of 60 per cent of the first year students at Kingshurst (114 students), but in this case nine of the students left the questions about their parents' occupations blank, sometimes putting comments such as 'too nosey' against them. A further two students gave answers too vague to be able to make a sensible classification. In other cases one answer could be classified, while the other could not. Table 6.2 shows the percentages of adults in each classification as described by these second intake year students.

It is most important not to take the exact numbers too seriously; however, there is an interesting overall difference between the distributions given in Table 6.1 and 6.2. This second intake year appears to have a slightly higher percentage of parents in social classes I and II than did the first intake year. The percentage from social classes IV and V still far outweighs the percentage from social classes I and II, but there would seem to be a significant increase in the number of men with professional occupations. In this sample from the second intake year there is a sprinkling of accountants, doctors, teachers, further education lecturers and similar, who were not found in the sample from the original intake year. This difference between the intakes of the two years should not be overstated, for parents with skilled manual and non-manual occupations still easily predominate. The proportion from professional homes in the second intake year is still small, and it cannot be said that the middle class have made any significant inroads into the CTC as various critical commentators such as Morrell (1989),

Table 6.2 Social class of parents of second intake year students (percentages)

	I	II	IIIN	IIIM	IV	V	Unemp.	House-worker	Student
Men N = 91	5	15	9	42	20	3	3	1	1
Women N = 100	1	10	31	7	17	8	2	21	3

Simon (1988) and Walford (1990a; 1990b) had predicted. The slight change must also be seen to be in agreement with the Principal's desire to attract a range of children with different social class backgrounds to the CTC. Finally, if those classified as unemployed and as houseworkers are taken together, there is practically the same proportion not in paid employment in both years.

Are the choosers chosen?

Social class is an important indicator of whether or not the CTC is accepting children from a range of different backgrounds and family circumstances, but there are other aspects worthy of consideration as well. In their study of the Assisted Places Scheme Edwards *et al.* (1989: 215) argue that those children and parents with the cultural and political resources necessary to gain an assisted place were also those likely to be able to ensure that their child would have obtained a place at a well-regarded state-maintained school anyway. There was evidence that those who obtained an assisted place would not have simply accepted their nearest local authority school, but would have sought for their child a maintained or alternative private school with a good reputation. To what extent were the parents of students at the CTC likely to have made alternative positive choices for their children had they not been accepted into the CTC?

Again, the information obtained from interviews and questionnaires has relevance. The students were all asked what school they would have attended had they not been accepted by the CTC, and were also asked about their own primary schools and the schools attended by any siblings. From this information an indication of the *minimum* proportion of children and parents who would have made active choices can be estimated. This active choice is most easily shown for those families living in north Solihull, which allocates children to schools on a catchment area basis, and where parents have to make an objection to that allocation. Without having access to the addresses of each pupil it is not possible to check whether each school stated to have been the alternative to the CTC was actually the catchment area school or another choice. But some schools named by the children would always require their parents to have made an active choice.

The Heart of England School, for example, is situated in the south-east of Solihull Borough about eight miles from the CTC –

well outside the catchment area – but is only three or four stations away from the CTC catchment area on a direct rail link. It has a good reputation and attracts applications from beyond its own catchment area. For those living in north Solihull, attendance at the Heart of England School would necessitate considerable costs in time and money. Coleshill School, in nearby Warwickshire, is also favoured by some parents over local north Solihull Schools, but here the costs are lower as it is nearer to the alternative north Solihull schools. To obtain admission to the King Edward's Grammar Schools within Birmingham, parents have to apply for their child to take the appropriate examination. As explained in Chapter 2, this group of voluntary aided schools is highly regarded, and to have turned down a place at one of these schools shows a considerable act of faith on the part of parents and children. Table 6.3 shows the percentage of each sample year group who stated that they would have attended these other schools.

The table shows that at least 8 per cent of parents and children within each year group would have chosen these three schools rather than their allocated LEA school. In practice, as the question asked 'What school would you have gone to if you had not got into the CTC?' those taking the King Edward's examination and not obtaining a place may not have given this information. From other information, the percentage actually applying to King Edward's was at least double the numbers given. Table 6.3 also shows that 3 per cent of the second intake year stated that they would have gone to a private school had they not been accepted by the CTC. As it happens, all three of these students who stated that they would have attended a private school have benefited from changes in the CTC's catchment area policy. From evidence about primary schools it is possible to discover that two of these students are part of the 5 per cent taken from outside the catchment area and one has taken advantage of the boundary changes to the catchment area. These changes for the second intake year have thus

Table 6.3 Schools that Kingshurst students would have attended (percentages)

	Heart of England	Coleshill	King Edward's	Private	Alternative school
First intake	5	1	2	0	14
Second intake	5	2	2	3	10

brought an increase not only in the number of middle-class parents, but also in the nuber using the CTC as an alternative to the private sector. Once again, the change should not be overstated as the numbers involved are small.

The final column on Table 6.3 tries to give a lower boundary to the number of parents and children actively seeking a choice of school. It shows the number of times students stated that they would have attended one individual named school, yet information on siblings indicated that the family had previously used another school. It is a very crude measure, which assumes that no active decision was made on behalf of older siblings, but it does give an indication of the *minimum* proportion of children and parents who were actively involved in making a choice of schools. Overall, the figures indicate that more than 20 per cent of the intake would not have automatically accepted their allocated LEA school. From other less systematic information it is known that the real percentage is actually far higher than this. About 40 per cent of those attending Archbishop Grimshaw RC Comprehensive School are not themselves Catholic, and about 20 per cent of the students selected for the CTC stated that they would have attended that school. Many of these were known to be non-Catholics. However, it is noticeable that at least some students stated that they would have attended each of the LEA schools within the catchment area. Generally there was a good spread of schools, but with only two in the second year saying that they would have attended Simon Digby School. None of the first years gave this choice as, by that time, the school was under threat of closure.

It would appear that there is a fairly high level of choice being exercised by these parents and children. But, of course, this does not mean that this level of choice would have existed in the absence of the CTC. It might well be argued that the introduction of the choice to apply to the CTC might well have acted to encourage parents to think about other possible choices as well. Indeed this is one of the catalyst effects that the CTCs claim to engender.

The experience of being selected

Not all of us are as cynical as Groucho Marx, who felt disdain for any club which would accept him as a member. Most of us are pleased to be selected by any restricted entry organization we apply to join. I did not ask the students any questions specifically about the effect that being chosen had on them, but their answers to several other questions revealed a number of interesting attitudes and confusions.

At the start of this chapter Nigel made it clear that he realized that the CTC takes children with a range of abilities. Yet students also recognize that the college is selective, and it is difficult for many of them to separate selection as such from selection by ability. Jayne, Tammie and Kirsty's comments were not unusual.

> Jayne: I thought I'd try for it, but I didn't think I'd get in.
> GW: Didn't you? Why not?
> Jayne: Because there were lots of people going for it, the ones who were all the brainy people, and I'm not . . . well I'm all right, but . . .
>
> Tammie: We had a bus come round to the school, and I went on it after school with my mum. And it looked really good, so I thought I'd have a go. I didn't think I'd get in because of the standards being so high.
>
> Kirsty: Some people think that you've got to be brainy to get into the school. Well, I wasn't that brainy.

At one level, all of these students know that the CTC took children with a wide range of abilities, yet they were muddled about the difference between selection and selection by ability: They were not alone. Sarah and others talked about 'passing the test' to get to the CTC, while others stated that they were very pleased to have 'passed'. This is to be expected, for, if applicants and their parents are interviewed for a restricted number of places and the children take a test, when they are offered a place, their experience is likely to be that they have 'passed'. It is worth noting that some adults also showed this confusion between selection and selection by ability. At one of the CTC open evenings, one parent called the CTCs 'the new grammar schools'. He was firmly corrected by Valerie Bragg, yet other parents had appeared to agree with his description. Each year, after the list of children accepted is announced, the Principal faces a flood of irate, confused and bitterly disappointed parents whose children have been refused entry. Many parents find it difficult to understand that their child has not been given a place, when they know of individual less able children from the same primary school who have been accepted.

In contrast, to have been accepted by the CTC made those students feel good about themselves. This was most clearly expressed by Jonathan, who categorically told me:

> It's important to me because I know that it's really, really hard to get in this school – and I've got into it. And that's an achievement to get into the school, and to know that there's hundreds of people who have just been let down. And I know that's an achievement for me to get in.

This was the most clearly expressed example from the forty-five interviews of the feelings of many of the students. They may not necessarily have seen their acceptance as 'an achievement' or even as 'passing', but it was a clear indication that *they* were wanted while others were not. Many of the students had primary school friends who had applied to the CTC but had not been offered a place. They had. They had been excited when they had first been told that they were going to be able to go to the CTC. They had looked forward to attending, and some could 'hardly wait' to start. In some ways, the fact that selection was not made on clear-cut criteria meant that students might even feel that it was the whole of them that was being selected – it was not necessarily that they were better academically, it was that they were better people.

In fairness, it should be stated that not all of the students saw their acceptance in this light. Some were simply mystified as to why they had been selected. Zoe had been told something else:

> GW: Why do you think you were selected?
> Zoe: I don't know. Mum asked the lady if I had a lot of chance, and the lady said that the names were just picked out of a hat, so really I think I was just lucky.

This is not actually correct. Names are not 'picked out of a hat', but such a statement obviously lessens the potential pain of not being offered a place. It also has the effect of lessening a student's feeling of being 'special' if accepted.

That being selected is usually good for those who have been selected is well known from many studies of the old system of grammar schools and secondary moderns which has been largely replaced by a comprehensive system (see for example Hargreaves 1967; Lacey 1970). The main problem, then and now, is the

possible detrimental effect on those who are not selected. I asked
students about friends at primary school and where they were now.
Several told me about their friends who 'didn't pass' or who had
'failed' or had been 'turned down' by the CTC. It is difficult to
believe that these children themselves did not interpret their experience in the same way. Although some of those not accepted
may have sat the Birmingham Grammar Schools' entrance test, for
many of them it was probably the first real interview of their lives.
They and their parents had made a distinct choice to try to attend
the CTC – and they had failed.

A national study of CTCs will investigate this aspect of selection further (Whitty *et al.* forthcoming), for it is intended that
parents and children who were not offered a place at a CTC will be
interviewed. However, the interviews with students in this study at
Kingshurst give some indications of possibilities. In the interviews I
did not ask specifically about relationships with other schools but
several of the students interviewed thought that it was important
that I knew. Their answers about what was 'special' about the
school were very varied and informative. Jonathan told me about
the verbal confrontations that CTC students sometimes had with
children from local schools. Edmund explained similar problems:

> People go on about it being the 'posh school', you know, and
> what the fuck? What are they on about when they say the
> 'posh school'? You know, people come up to you and say
> 'You go to the posh school don't you? – the computer
> school'. They say we're always on the computers, but we're
> not. I just say it's like a normal school, but maybe better. At
> the beginning of last year, and to the middle as well, we did
> have a bit of a problem from [a local school]. At the bus stops,
> going home, we did have a bit of trouble. They were sup-
> posed to be coming down here to beat us all up – but they
> never turned up. We were lucky there!

Of course, this might just be an example of the sort of rivalry
between schools that is unfortunately all too common. But some
students made it clear that they felt there was more to the animosity that this. James, for example, explained the problems between schools as follows.

James: A lot of my friends at [a nearby school] say 'It's rubbish at your school'. And I say, 'How would you know, you've never been there', and they just go quiet. And all these other schools that are threatening that they're going to come to the gates and get us, and some of the kids wait behind, but nobody ever turns up. They keep threatening us that they're going to get us, but they never turn up.

GW: Do you get name-calling as well, or what?

James: Sometimes, but that's the time you've got your jackets on anyway, so they can't see where you're from. In the summer-time you get more name calling, but I don't take much notice.

GW: Is that older pupils or people your own age?

James: Own age, the older pupils don't really bother, because they couldn't get in anyway.

GW: Do you think it's because they didn't get in?

James: Yes, because I know four of them that didn't get in, and they're the ones that often call kids names.

Even more surprising was an unsolicited comment from Joanna who, after saying how much she enjoyed being at the CTC, launched into an account of the activities of the mother of a girl who used to be her best friend but who had not been offered a place at the CTC.

> Well, Claire, who went in for the school, her mum's been saying that she wouldn't send Kevin, that's the younger brother, to the school. I mean – 'It's a horrible school and the hours are too long', and everything. She's spreading it round about it. But my mum puts her right, saying that it's better than some other schools, and all that.

Such comments from students interviewed were supported by casual conversations that I had with students over my time at the CTC. It was certainly not that there was great warfare between the CTC and other schools. In fact, it was significant that the same few tales were told by several students, rather than there being a range of incidents. But, on the other hand, students were sometimes teased and threatened by children from other schools, and some of them believed that their aggressors were especially those who had not been selected. In the last quote there is voiced the possibility that 'failing' to obtain a place may affect parents as well as children because, of course, parents are interviewed alongside their children. It is not unlikely that parents whose child is not admitted feel some of the pain of failure as well as the child. They may also feel that part of that failure was their own fault. Was it their own inadequacies that led their child to 'fail'? These are all speculations, but what is clear is that the potential for children to become labelled as having 'passed' or to have 'failed' is present in the CTC selection procedure. Selection is based on unclear criteria rather than academic ability but the positive and negative aspects of selection still accompany the process.

7

Reactions and responses

Introduction

The last few chapters have described and discussed various aspects of the City Technology College, Kingshurst, from the inside. In this chapter we move beyond the college itself and examine some of the range and types of responses by others to the establishment of a CTC at Kingshurst. In particular we look at responses in nearby schools and in local industry and commerce.

One of the main objectives of the research on The CTC Kingshurst was to try to determine the effect of the college on nearby schools and its impact on education and training for the local community. Information was gained on the effects of the CTC on the local schools' system by interviewing most of the Headteachers of the local secondary school, along with some of the teachers and children in those schools. Short visits to the schools were made, which included some periods of classroom observation, and a number of local education authority officials within Solihull and Birmingham were also interviewed. To attempt some assessment of the effects of the CTC on education and training within the local community generally, press coverage was followed and local politicians were interviewed. Finally, a sample of representatives of local employers who might be expected to wish to make contact with the college was interviewed.

The most evident and important finding from all of this research was that the CTC was but one of many influences on local schools and on the community, at a time of rapid change. These major influences included the Technical and Vocational Education Initiative which had been in operation since the early 1980s, the changes in powers of governing bodies as a result of the 1986 Education Act, the imposition of new teachers' contracts and conditions of service and, of greatest importance, the restructuring of the education system enacted through the 1988 Education Reform Act. When the CTC proposals were announced in 1986, there was little indication that they would be rapidly followed by plans for a National Curriculum, open enrolment, local management of schools, and grant-maintained schools – each or which, by itself, would have a far greater effect on local education provision than a single CTC could possibly have. The CTCs had been introduced, in part, to increase competition between schools and as a step towards a privatized system, but the 1988 Education Reform Act made the CTCs only a small part of a much wider restructuring. During the time of the research, each LEA had to restructure its activities rapidly, produce funding formulae for its schools in preparation for local management of schools, and develop ways of dealing with the National Curriculum. Birmingham had the added problems of dealing with a legal attack for its unequal provision of grammar school places for boys and girls, and the opting out of two of its schools to become grant maintained. At such a rapid time of change, the effect of one CTC, sited in Solihull, was just a minor irritation to Birmingham LEA in comparison to the need to deal with change within its own nearby 500 schools.

Both Birmingham and Solihull were also faced with falling school rolls at the secondary level and the government's demand that a large percentage of the resultant over-capacity of school places be removed as quickly as possible. School closures, and the threat of school closures, were a prominent feature of the educational landscape. With falling school rolls and budgets largely dependent upon actual pupil numbers, competition between LEA schools and all that this entails was almost inevitable. The presence of the CTC was just one more coloured thread in the complicated tapestry of change. Its effect on the overall picture is very difficult to perceive accurately once it was in place.

Complexity is thus the major feature of any description of the possible effects of the CTC on local schools and the local education and training community.

Responses in local schools

Perhaps the most obvious effect of introducing a new CTC into an existing system of county and voluntary aided comprehensive schools is that children selected for that CTC are taken out of the LEA maintained sector. It was shown in Chapter 2 that the secondary school age population in north Solihull reached its peak in 1983 and then rapidly declined. The LEA dealt with this peak in demand by temporarily using the buildings of an old school in neighbouring Birmingham, and adjusted to the subsequent decline by closing Kingshurst school. The re-use of the Kingshurst site as a CTC would inevitably put pressure on LEA schools in the borough by reducing the potential number of pupils in the age range. The LEA's well-planned management of falling school rolls was immediately put into question, and it appeared that a further school might have to close as a result of the CTC taking pupils.

It is thus inevitable that the initial reaction of Heads and teachers in local schools to the announcement that a CTC was to open in their area was that of surprise, shock and anger. On interview one of the Heads said that he had been astonished that the area was to have a CTC for, although it had its social problems, it was not in the inner city, and several other areas in the West Midlands were clearly far more suitable. At a point when they were already facing severe falling rolls, the local Heads feared for the continued health, and possibly survival, of their own schools. In particular, they saw the possibility of highly motivated children and parents being taken from their schools by the CTC, and argued that, in competition with the CTC, the odds were stacked unfairly against them. In early 1987, when the Kingshurst site was selected, several of the Heads publicly expressed their outrage on radio, television and in newspaper reports. Later in that year, the Heads of the two groups of schools in east Birmingham and north Solihull took some united action against the CTC through increased advertising.

In both east Birmingham and north Solihull the strategy adopted by the Heads for the 1988 intake was to increase the advertising material going to homes in the area and to present a united and collaborative image of the LEA schools. Individual schools were not to be seen as competing between themselves for students, but as presenting a common front against the competition from the CTC. In east Birmingham the four schools and the East Birmingham

College were given extra funding by Birmingham LEA to produce an A4 coloured folder, which was distributed to all families with a child about to transfer schools. The folder presented the image of 'Serving you and your community', and emphasized a tradition of caring for Birmingham children, community involvement, meeting local needs, firm links with primary schools, work-experience schemes and co-operation between the four schools and East Birmingham College to offer 'the widest possible range of A levels' and BTEC courses. The folder included separate leaflets on the individual schools, each presented in the same format. There was no explicit mention of the CTC, but the folder carefully countered many of the advantages that it was thought the CTC might have over the LEA schools, and was widely known as the 'Anti-CTC Brochure'. Of the eighteen photographs, four showed computers, three showed engineering equipment, two were of science lessons, and one of a recording studio. However, the illustrations also showed dance, music, art and a well-stocked library. The folder had the message that it was 'Supported by Land Rover' together with the Land Rover logo printed on the back.

In north Solihull the Heads of the five schools organized a similar campaign to advertise themselves. Somewhat ironically, they obtained extra funding from Solihull Education Department specifically to produce a leaflet to counter the effect of the CTC which the local authority itself had allowed to be established. Their leaflet was smaller than that of east Birmingham, but it was delivered to every household in the area in the same way as was the CTC leaflet. Somewhat controversially, the delivery included some homes in Birmingham and nearby Warwickshire as well as the whole of the Solihull part of the CTC catchment area. Again, it was in full colour with photographs showing music, drama and sports, as well as technology and industry links. The CTC was not mentioned, but one picture showed students outside the ubiquitous Land Rover factory. The emphasis of the leaflet was 'traditional standards' and 'tomorrow's skills', and the final page included the headline 'We still put people before technology'.

This joint response to the CTC from each of the two groups of schools occurred only for the 1988 intake. By 1989 within north Solihull, there was pressure to close another school and the Heads had become more individually competitive. With falling rolls and two schools dangerously small, the Heads no longer wished to produce a combined leaflet, but produced their own publicity in competition with each other as well as the CTC. Meanwhile, the Heads of those Birmingham schools not directly affected by the CTC had complained about the extra funding and advertising being provided for the east Birmingham schools within the CTC catchment area. They demanded equal publicity for all schools in the borough. The result of their protest was that a huge pile of joint leaflets printed for the 1989 intake was never distributed.

These two leaflets have been described in detail, not because they were particularly significant in the long run, but because their production and distribution was one of the few activities of the LEA schools that can unambiguously be seen as a direct response to the CTC. Since that time the educational climate has changed dramatically, and a greatly increased competitiveness between schools has been introduced through the 1988 Education Reform Act, with open admissions in LEA schools, the option for schools to become grant maintained and the corresponding removal of the LEA's ability to plan pupil numbers. The result is that while there have been very many changes within the LEA schools in the CTC catchment area, this is also true for practically all other secondary schools in the country, and it is impossible to establish the extent to which most of these changes were the response to the CTC, rather than to other wider structural changes.

One of the major areas where all Heads stated that there had been an increase in activity in the last couple of years was in the marketing of their schools. Several of the Heads have now given communications and public relations a high profile within their schools and have made this a position of special responsibility within the school hierarchy. To take just one school as an example, Smith's Wood School in north Solihull gave a temporary increment to a teacher who was responsible for this area. In 1987 the school introduced an Open Week where parents could come to the school unannounced to see the school in action. That same year it also started a regular desk-top published Newsletter for parents. The following year, in addition to publishing the statutory information required, it produced a twenty-page A5 self-promotional brochure, with black and white and colour pictures, costing about £1 each. Links with feeder primary schools have been strengthened, with regular cluster meetings, days when secondary teachers visit the primaries and vice versa, and visits by primary pupils to the school. Far greater effort is made to get school events reported in local newspapers and on local radio.

Park Hall is another good example. It consciously uses a wide variety of marketing techniques, and niche markets on science, technology and industry links. It targets publicity in a planned way, using local and national press, radio and television. Events are organized in such a way that media coverage can be achieved. The school not only has the usual open days and evenings when prospective parents and children visit, but also organizes a 'roadshow' of teachers, pupils and equipment to visit local primary schools. This involves talks from senior teachers, and a couple of 'fun' lessons for primary pupils. Separate teachers are given responsibility for local press, open days and roadshows, while the Head handles national marketing – to target Kenneth Baker to present publicly one of the Park Hall/Land Rover certificates requires considerable skill! Leaflets and the prospectus form another part of Park Hall's strategy. The school's prospectus consists of eighteen A4 pages. The majority are typewritten and duplicated, but two pages are printed with colour photographs. The sheets are contained within a stylish and expensively printed folder, which has a cut-out to reveal one of the photographs. In 1988 the school spent over £1,000 on such printing – more than £4 per intake student.

Similar increases in the amount of effort and funding spent on marketing were reported by most of the schools. Simon Digby School produced a promotional video. Byng Kendrick Central School now has its name in letters a metre high along the top of its main teaching building which faces the road. All of the schools regard links with primary schools to be of major importance. They all have regular cluster meetings with feeder primary schools and shared INSET days. The Park Hall cluster, for example, has used some of these joint meetings to develop a profiling system which runs from 5 to 16 for the pupils which move from feeder schools to Park Hall. Profiling had originally developed as part of the school's TVEI scheme, but the development downwards of positive pupil-generated profiles has the additional advantage of drawing the feeder schools nearer to the secondary. These links are maintained through visits to Heads the top-junior teachers in each of the feeder schools; they also receive a copy of the lower-school information booklet.

The schools were clear that this growing emphasis on market-ing had increased in the last few years, but argued that the CTC was not the major cause. In particular, as the area was one of rapidly declining secondary school rolls, where one school was likely to close, competition was almost inevitable once parents

were given greater freedom of choice of school. Full local management of schools and open enrolment would have automatically led
to greater competition between schools in north Solihull and east
Birmingham, as it has in many other areas throughout the country.
The extra effect that the CTC has had on this competition is very
difficult to assess, but is probably small. One Head admitted that it
might have 'focused our attention more', while another stated that
it was 'an added factor'. In contrast, one Head stated that there was
no doubt in his mind that the increased attention that his school
gave to visits from feeder primary schools was due to the presence
of the CTC. In some cases, the nature of the promotional material
also appeared to be influenced by CTC material. Simon Digby's
advertising leaflet, for example, had comments from pupils very
similar to the CTC's 'Seal of Approval' messages from students in
its prospectus, while Sir Wilfrid Martineau and Whitesmore's
materials also emphasized a pupil's perspective.

In general, Heads and teachers accepted this increase in competition, but they complained that competition against the CTC
was fundamentally unfair. One closely involved teacher explained:

> This competition was not like selling eggs, for there was only
> a certain number of kids who could come to any of the
> schools. There is not an unlimited market. You can't create
> any more demand, you can only share out the pupil numbers
> in a different way. We have declining rolls, so the schools are
> simply 'scrabbling around' for their pupils. Now this school
> can advertise, and it can try to get more pupils, but the
> competition is unfair. We get no extra money for advertising;
> it has to be taken out of capitation. It really annoys me that
> the CTC has redirected resources away from what is really
> important in education, and into marketing. It's not that I'm
> against letting people know what the school is doing. That is
> just and right, but I object to so much money and effort going
> into PR. The problem is that the CTC has far more money to
> spend on PR than we have, or any other local school. Ken-
> neth Baker can't afford to let the CTC fail, so if we and others
> are successful in our advertising, the CTC will simply up its
> own advertising way beyond what we can afford in an at-
> tempt to get more children.

Another teacher argued that this was Kenneth Baker's 'bid for
fame' and 'swoop for glory', and that he could not let the CTC fail.

If it looked to be in trouble, then the rules would be simply changed to make sure it could be seen as a success. This teacher saw the changes to the catchment area in this light, as the numbers applying in the first year had not been particularly high.

While the schools were prepared to admit that the CTC might have had some slight effect on marketing methods, all of the Solihull schools claimed that the CTC had not affected their curriculum in any direct way. They saw their increased involvement in industrial links, science and technology, for example, as developing from earlier TVEI schemes and from TVE Extension, and not as being related to the CTC, but to other changes. At Smith's Wood a new first year foundation course was started in 1987. Its aim was to smooth the transfer process from primary to secondary by having about half of the timetable for each class in the first year taught by one teacher only. The Head explained that the development work needed for this change could occur only once the lengthy teacher action of the mid-1980s had ended. It was that change in circumstances that was much more important than the arrival of the CTC on the scene. Another example is the double GCSE in business structures and technology that was jointly developed by Smith's Wood, Simon Digby and Park Hall. This new and unique modular course started in 1988 and pooled teaching skills and resources between the three schools, but was seen as the direct result of TVE Extension. In 1989 the Head of Park Hall explained:

> At the end of the day, what we are doing here and what we have done, is the result of what we have been doing over the last five years, and our work with industry and the way we've been thinking about it. I mean, the CTC has had a zero effect on the curriculum. What has had far more effect is our work with industry, the proposal for TVEI extension, and the proposals for the National Curriculum – they're the ones we've been looking at. The CTC is neither here nor there really. I don't know what they're doing. At the moment, I don't care what they're doing – we're too busy.

This lack of knowledge about what the CTC was actually doing was echoed by other Heads and teachers in the neighbouring secondary schools. For most of the schools, the only contact with the CTC was through sports fixtures. Even though the Heads shared membership of the Secondary Heads Association with Valerie Bragg they had no contact with her, neither side having taken any initiative to meet. There had been no visits to the CTC by Heads, and no visits by CTC staff to other secondary schools. It was difficult to see how any dissemination of ideas from the CTC could occur when there was so little contact.

Although the schools did not feel that the CTC had affected what they were doing in any direct way other than marketing, some of the industrialists involved with both the CTC and the other local schools felt that it had. These industrialists claimed that the CTC had been very specific about what it wanted from them, which they appreciated. They did not want to waste their time, and preferred clear, well-thought-through demands. They wanted demands to be made on them, and they felt that working with the CTC had shown them various ways in which they could be useful, which they had then passed on to the other schools.

Pupil numbers

The real and potential effects of the CTC on other nearby schools can be understood only in the context of local falling secondary school rolls. The dramatic decline in pupil numbers is illustrated in Table 7.1, which shows the number of pupils on roll in the nine schools in the CTC catchment area for the years from 1981 until 1989.

Table 7.1   Pupil numbers on roll in September 1981–9

	1981	1982	1983	1984	1985	1986	1987	1988	1989
East Birmingham									
Byng Kendrick	984	954	936	918	934	901	818	706	594
Sir Wilfrid's	1,216	1,190	1,201	1,224	1,242	1,232	1,202	1,189	1,187
Sheldon Heath	1,663	1,632	1,645	1,628	1,652	1,514	1,353	1,196	1,115
Cockshut Hill	1,302	1,282	1,303	1,335	1,317	1,315	1,315	1,336	1,335
North Solihull									
Park Hall	1,481	—	—	—	1,482	1,411	1,380	1,335	1,320
Smith's Wood	1,411	—	—	—	1,264	1,177	1,035	869	726
Archbishop Grimshaw RC	1,164	—	—	—	1,316	1,299	1,275	1,245	1,143
Whitesmore	1,233	—	—	—	968	890	789	710	608
Simon Digby	1,090	—	—	—	706	623	556	450	373
Kingshurst	1,186	—	—	—	—	343	147	—	—
Culey Green	303	—	—	—	—	181	71	—	—
CTC								180	360

Note: Some data missing

The most important feature of the table is the dramatic decline in pupil numbers within the schools in the CTC catchment area as a whole from about 13,000 in 1981 to 8,700 in 1989. These numbers include a gradual increase in the numbers of pupils staying on after 16, so the figures are not a direct measure of the number of children in the area. The small numbers of children attending private schools are also excluded, as are the Birmingham children throughout the period who were selected to attend the grammar schools and, more recently, all children who have chosen to attend LEA schools outside their area of residence, including those in different LEAs. The table includes those living outside the catchment area who attended the schools within that boundary. However, the general picture is that of a very great decline in the numbers of children in the CTC catchment area schools. The CTC has just added a further problem for the LEAs to deal with. Each year after September 1988 about 170 children who would have attended these schools will attend the CTC instead. The figures in Table 7.1 take account of only the first two years' intake to the CTC in 1988 and 1989. From 1990 to 1992 three more groups of about 170 will be removed from the LEA sector. On average each school in the catchment area will be about one class smaller than it would otherwise have been. In addition, from 1990, the CTC will be recruiting students to its post-16 courses, and will take perhaps another 300–400 students over the two years who might otherwise have been in the state sector.

In practice, Table 7.1 shows that some schools have been affected more than others by the opening of the CTC in September 1988, because there is a preference order for schools. Some popular schools, such as Cockshut Hill, receive more first choices than they can take: in spring 1990 there were 350 applications for 241 places, and the Head was able to claim in a *Birmingham Evening Mail* report of 5 April:

> This shows again that parents do want the high standards and well-disciplined ethos of an established school. Experience and tradition count for a lot. We've been oversubscribed in former years, but this is the highest ever. We're not all that well endowed in the facilities. Parents don't send their children here for the facilities – therefore they must send them for the things that matter most. The school is known for its high standards and for exam results. It's a uniformed school with

old-fashioned ideas about standards and behaviour. The school was thriving despite a City Technology College leaflet campaign in the Cockshut Hill catchment area.

If this Head of a thriving school felt the need to attack the CTC in this way, it is likely that feelings in schools at the other end of the popularity spectrum felt even stronger anger. Simon Digby and Byng Kendrick, for example, both lost two intake classes in the first year of the CTC's operation, and staff at these schools put the blame firmly on the CTC. However, Table 7.1 shows that the effect of the CTC was on top of that of falling rolls and greater parental choice and can be devastating for a less popular school. In 1988, for example, Smith's Wood's intake numbers were only about thirty lower than the previous year, but the numbers entering at the bottom of the school were far smaller than the numbers leaving who had entered five years earlier. As a result, in 1989 ten staff members were lost (from 60.5), with two of these at most being attributable to the CTC in that year.

Pupil numbers are only part of the story. Teachers and Head-teachers in the LEA schools were almost unanimous in their condemnation of the way in which the CTC selected students, and most perceived that the comprehensiveness of their own schools was suffering as a direct result of the CTC. Most of the Heads did not believe that the CTC took children with a representative range of academic abilities, but they were certain that, even if this was true, the CTC was selecting children who were gifted in other areas. They felt that, where the CTC was selecting children of lower ability, those children were disproportionately likely to be good at something like sport, drama, art or music. They felt that the CTC was likely to select well-disciplined and motivated children, and reject any potential problem children, leaving them for the LEA schools to deal with. Of course, they also recognized that the CTC would not often have to reject such children, for the application process meant that these children would be unlikely to apply. Only the well-motivated parents and pupils would apply to the CTC, and these Heads believed that the selection process was thus likely to take from the LEA system many parents who might form the backbone of supporters for their own schools.

In Chapter 6 it was shown that it is correct to assume that the application and interview process used by the CTC is likely to take from the LEA schools many of the well-motivated pupils and parents and some pupils with special gifts. Indeed, the original DES document of 1986 made it explicit that motivation was to be used as a basis for selection. The children have to be well motivated to accept the longer school day and term, the higher amounts of work that are expected of them and the commitment to education or training until the age of 18. It is just this type of student that is so important to any school, and which the CTC is taking from the LEA system.

The resulting effect of the CTC on staff morale in the LEA schools is impossible to measure. The staff in the less popular schools recognized that the CTC was not the only cause of their problems but also that it was inevitable that the CTC would be the recipient of much of the animosity. In general, they saw it as simply madness that a new, well-equipped school should be opened in an area where schools were under-subscribed, and where they knew their own schools could be improved with just a small part of the extra finance involved. Faced with cuts in staff-ing in response to declining pupil numbers and uncertainty about their own futures, staff were generally angry at the situation they found themselves in. Many of the staff felt that their own work over the years was being undervalued, and their schools unjustly criticized.

This level of anger and concern was not restricted to the less popular schools, for even the more popular schools were worried about the future of their sixth form provision. It was expected that the start of the CTC's post-16 provision in 1990 would take some students away from the LEA sixth forms and produce new diffi-culties. Heads did not expect large numbers of their pupils to make this move, but a few pupils leaving could make particular subjects unviable and thus threaten the whole shape of their provision. It was a special irony that some of the schools likely to be affected by the CTC's post-16 plans were those which had spearheaded BTEC provision in the area before the CTC plan was even proposed.

The closure of Simon Digby School

In October 1988 Solihull LEA decided to enter a period of con-sultation on the closure of Simon Digby School, which many argued was the direct result of opening the CTC. At first sight there is an appealing logic to the argument that if Kingshurst

Secondary School was originally closed because of falling school rolls, and then opens again in a new guise, another school must close in its place. In practice the situation is rather more complex than this in three separate ways. First, the CTC draws its students from Birmingham as well as Solihull, so does not take as many students from the other north Solihull schools as the original LEA school. Second, there have been changes in the secondary age population structure since the original decision was made. Third, the political balance of power between individual schools and LEAs has changed as a result of the 1988 Education Reform Act.

Table 7.2 displays the actual number of pupils aged 11–16 on roll in each of the schools from 1986 to 1989, as well as the estimates of future numbers which were used by Solihull LEA in their decision to close Simon Digby school (Solihull Education Committee, 22 March 1989). The figures were presented in a slightly different form at the two relevant Education Committee meetings, and the totals for the actual numbers on roll do not include about 100 children in 1988 who were already attending the CTC from Solihull. The figures for total numbers are correct for 1994 onwards. The predicted numbers from January 1990 onwards are based upon September 1988 figures, and are calculated assuming that the CTC takes a further 400 pupils from the Solihull part of the catchment area. In addition to these pupils, in the period 1986–9 there were respectively 308, 308, 338 and 347 post-16 pupils in the north Solihull schools. Most of these pupils were in Archbishop Grimshaw RC School or Park Hall, with a very few in Whitesmore.

Table 7.2   Pupil numbers in north Solihull (11–16 only)

| | Actuals (Sept.) | | | 1988 Estimates (Jan.) | | | | | |
	1986	1987	1988	1990	1991	1992	1993	1994	1995
Park Hall	1,317	1,262	1,216	1,175	1,186	1,187	1,170	1,180	1,175
Smith's Wood	1,191	1,049	875	727	671	645	643	715	788
Whitesmore	862	805	708	619	586	569	552	605	658
Simon Digby	623	555	458	386	354	340	346	395	439
Archbishop Grimshaw RC	1,154	1,119	1,074	976	935	926	908	935	950
Kingshurst	343	147							
Culey Green	181	71							
Total	5,671	5,008	4,331	3,883	3,732	3,667	3,619	3,830	4,010

The exact number of places available in each school is a function of the method of calculation. In the information presented to the Education Committee in October 1988, the Director of Education for Solihull chose to use the DES-approved design size for permanent accommodation and temporary classroom capacity of twenty-five places. Using this method of calculation, he estimated that the accommodation available in the five secondary schools for 11–16 year olds at September 1988 provided 6,375 places for a predicted number of 4,510 school age pupils in 1995 (including the 500 who will go to the CTC). Simon Digby School was shown as having a capacity of 1,200 pupils, so removing these places leaves 5,175 11–16 places for 4,510 pupils. In a similar way, using 1981 figures, the five schools provided a total of 7,125 places for all ages in permanent and temporary accommodation, with 6,850 places in permanent accommodation. The removal of Simon Digby's 1,200 places still leaves the area with 5,650 permanent places and 275 temporary places for 4,510 11–16 pupils and about 350 post-16 students. In the information presented to the Education Committee in 1988, the Director of Education explained that even though there was an upturn in the number of younger children, the most optimistic calculations predicted that, unless a school was closed, there was likely to be a continuing over-supply of some 1,500 places for 11–16 even if the CTC had not existed. In practice, it was to be expected that by 1993 the CTC would be removing 500 students from the north Solihull system giving a total over-supply of some 2,000 places if no action was taken. Given that the government was pressing for greater efficiency and effectiveness in schooling, it was not unreasonable for the Education Committee to consider the closure of one of these schools.

Those who might wish to support the retention of all of the schools could argue that it would be better to have more space in secondary schools than the full capacity would imply, that health and safety regulations had changed since the schools were constructed, and that all temporary school accommodation should be removed. Alternative methods of calculating space give very different maximum numbers of pupils that could be accommodated, and the method chosen was amongst the most optimistic. For example, although Simon Digby school was originally designed to accommodate 1,200 children, the maximum number the school had ever held was 1,062 in 1972, and at that point it had also used an annexe to accommodate some of the younger children. It might also be argued that the schools could increase their sixth form provision; indeed, the figures do show some increase over the last few years.

The options open to the LEA in their attempts to deal with the problem of falling school rolls were severely restricted. Changes within the 1988 Education Reform Act made it illegal to impose lower admission limits than the capacity of each school, or to allocate pupils from the south of the borough (where the schools were fuller) to these north Solihull schools. Better marketing of the schools was felt desirable, but unlikely to make a significant difference to the overall numbers attracted from outside the borough. The other alternative was to close one of the schools. Of the five schools, Simon Digby and Whitesmore were the most likely candidates for closure. Simon Digby, which had the lowest number of pupils, a lower level of occupancy, and fewer first preferences from parents and pupils than Whitesmore, was selected for consultation on closure.

The closure was heavily contested. The three separate consultation meetings with staff, governors and parents were all well attended and vociferous. Those involved in opposing closure demonstrated, walked, canvassed, petitioned and argued their case with local and national politicians. The Director of Education's report of 22 March 1989 summarizes the results of the consultation exercise, submissions from staff, governors and parents of the school, and from the Teaching Staff Joint Committee thus: 'there is unequivocal and resolute opposition to the closure of Simon Digby School'. The Director was also forced to admit in his report that there were strong arguments about the quality of the school in favour of retention.

> Its education/industry links are strong and well-developed; its external examination results registered an improvement in 1988; the number of pupils leaving the fifth-year without any examination qualifications has been reduced to 3 pupils; the school's TVE work in Media Technology has been especially successful, the school has developed impressive initiatives in Drama, together with outside links in this field, and pupil attendance levels have improved.
>
> (Report of Director of Education 22 March 1989)

A new Headteacher had been appointed in 1986, and he has admitted that the school had a poor reputation prior to his appointment. For example, due to four years of teacher action, which had been happening in Solihull a few years before it became national, the fourth year group had never had a parents' evening before the new Head took over. But changes had been made such that the morale of the school had risen, examination results improved and the school's reputation blossomed. By 1988 the school even had a regular column in one of the free newspapers.

Clearly the small size of Simon Digby – with 458 pupils in 1988 and even lower numbers predicted – was the decisive argument in favour of closure. In addition to the problems of staffing the curriculum, the school would have been graded as a small school which would have resulted in the addition of £100,000 each year in teacher costs. The drop in first year enrolments from eighty-seven in September 1987 to forty-five in September 1988 was a crucial turning-point, precipitating any moves which might have become necessary later. In September 1988 twenty-five children from within the nominal catchment area of Simon Digby went to the CTC instead. This number was roughly similar to that of pupils going to the CTC from Whitesmore or Smith's Wood, but Simon Digby started from a lower base than either of these schools and the effect was to reduce the intake to just two small classes. The actual role of the CTC in the process is difficult to unravel, for open enrolment and greater parental choice might have produced similar results a few years later as overall pupil numbers decreased, but parents and teachers clearly blamed the proposed closure on the CTC.

The reaction against closure was so great and the support for the school so strong that, when the LEA announced that it was going to seek closure, the school's governors decided to try to opt out of LEA control and become grant maintained instead. It was recognized that the chance of being allowed to opt out was slim, but that a government pushing for greater competition between schools might see some advantages in having a CTC and a grant-maintained school in the same area. It was also recognized that there had been fewer applications to opt out than had been expected, and that the government was anxious to encourage more schools to follow this path. The governors felt that if they could show a high level of parental support for the school they might have a chance.

In the event, there was a 76 per cent turn-out of parents, with 98 per cent voting in favour of grant-maintained status. The campaign continued throughout 1989, with first year admission numbers actually going up in September 1989, even though there was the threat of closure hanging over the school. However, the Secretary of State announced his decision in November 1989 that grant-maintained status would not be granted, mainly on the basis of size. The decision was not unexpected as it would have been the smallest of the grant-maintained schools at that time. The school will transfer its 1988 and 1989 intake pupils to other schools in September 1990 and finally close in 1992.

It is probably less likely that a school in Simon Digby's position would be scheduled for closure by an LEA now than it was in 1989. LEAs have learnt that there is a very real chance that such schools might be allowed to opt out of their control and thus inhibit future plans. In particular, a High Court action in Avon has made it clear that grant-maintained status can still be granted to a school scheduled for closure even when this disrupts LEA plans for reorganization of educational provision and harms other schools. As a result, since 1989 several authorities have shelved or modified plans to reorganize their provision in such a way that schools do not need to be closed, with the risk that they may seek grant-maintained status. In such a changed political climate, LEAs are likely to continue to maintain schools which they actually believe are too small to be viable, rather than risk a grant-maintained school in their area. They are likely to try to encourage a more even distribution of pupils between their schools to ensure that all of them maintain a reasonable school roll. In this situation, even though there was over-provision of places in Solihull, the existence of the CTC could have been crucial. Without the CTC, Simon Digby might have expected to have about 100 extra pupils in 1995 (its share of the north Solihull numbers), bringing its numbers to about 540. This might still have been viewed by the LEA as too small, but there are already some grant-maintained schools of this size, and they might not have been prepared to take the risk of trying to close it. Additionally, by this time the area would have been experiencing rising school rolls again, which would have made closing a school more difficult to argue for. In short, without the CTC, the decision to close Simon Digby might have been put back a couple of years, and this delay might have been long enough to have made closure unlikely.

The saga of Simon Digby does not end with the scheduled closure in 1992. One of the main reasons for closing the school was the need for efficient use of resources but, once the final closure plans for the school had been made, it became evident that there were going to be some unanticipated costs to the closure, which would continue for many years. The closure plan involves the transfer of all the 1988 and 1989 intake pupils to other Solihull schools, so that the school could close swiftly with less time for a deterioration in the school's atmosphere to take place. In practice, many of the parents and pupils decided that they would prefer to attend schools outside Solihull, in particular Coshill School in Warwickshire, which is less than a mile from Simon Digby on the other side of the M6 motorway. Solihull Education Department became concerned at the extra expense that the borough would incur in paying for these children in Warwickshire, and offered to provide free transport for all of the first and second year Simon Digby pupils to any school in Solihull. This unplanned extra expenditure will continue for another six years for some pupils. In addition, in order to maintain an adequate curriculum within Simon Digby for the two years from 1990 and to ensure that the school keeps an adequate staff until it finally closes, the Head has also managed to negotiate extra staffing and extra scale posts. In 1990/91 the school will have about 250 children and 28 staff giving a pupil/staff ratio of about 9:1.

A further paradoxical development is that there are plans to use the Simon Digby buildings to house a northern annexe to Solihull College of Technology. From September 1990 part of the buildings will be used for BTEC, Youth Training Schemes and other further education courses, and it is hoped that this will be extended once the school pupils finally leave in 1992. The present Head of the school has been able to encourage the fourth and fifth year students, who will remain at the school, with the idea that they will be taught within a more 'college-like' atmosphere for their last two years. The long-standing agreement between both of the major political parties in the borough that there was a need for a further education presence in the north is, rather belatedly, coming to fruition. The irony is that the Kingshurst buildings were at one point scheduled for this role, but the buildings were sold off instead to the CTC. The further education courses in the Simon Digby buildings will now compete directly with the private sector provision of similar courses in the CTC.

Employers' responses to The CTC Kingshurst

It has been shown earlier that the £1 million backing for the CTC Kingshurst from the international Hanson plc was of considerable importance to the whole CTC project, as it was the first major company to announce its support. Other major international companies such as ICI, Shell and BP had refused to support the CTC concept, and the Confederation of British Industry and the Industrial Society had both been very critical of the idea. Nevertheless, Kingshurst has managed to gather support from a wide range of sponsors at the local and national level, not only in terms of money and equipment, but also in providing executives to help plan the CTC, advise on a range of topics, give talks to students, and (in the future) give work experience placements and provide industrial tutors. This section explores the variety of reactions of local employers to the siting of the first CTC near to them. It draws upon several individual interviews with industrialists and a series of interviews with senior personnel in local industry and commerce in May–July 1989. These interviews were conducted by two postgraduate students at Aston University, Susan Phillips and Stephen Moss. Both of these studies were small scale and the samples cannot be considered to be representative of all employers, but they give an impression of the range and variety of responses in the local area.

The first study (Phillips 1989) involved sixteen businesses within the travel-to-work area of the CTC. There were approximately equal numbers of companies from the manufacturing and service sectors and a sample of small, medium and large companies within each sector. Nine companies employed over 1,000 people, five between 200 and 1,000, and two between 20 and 200. In each case the person with the greatest responsibility for implementing personnel policy was interviewed. The second study (Moss 1989) drew its sample from a list of public and private organizations in Birmingham and Solihull provided by the Birmingham Chamber of Commerce. Here ten senior and middle-range managers were interviewed within a range of organizations including a public utility, a council department, a bank, and an insurance company, as well as manufacturing industries and two large retail chains. In all, interviews were conducted in twenty-six organizations.

Of the sixteen companies in the first sample, seven reported that they had been approached by letter from the CTC asking for their support. Of the ten companies in the second sample, Lucas Industries had been involved at an early stage as one of the foundation sponsors, while the other nine claimed not to have been approached. The eight businesses which claimed to have been approached were four large manufacturing companies, two large service organizations, one of which was a medium-sized manufacturing company and the other a medium-sized service organization. Somewhat unexpectedly, all eight cases where an approach had been made were prepared to support the CTC in some way, either through gifts or by seconding staff. All of the manufacturing companies contributed financially (although sometimes not very generously), whereas only one of the service industries did so. One of the manufacturing industries expects to give only funding, but all of the others stated that they anticipated assisting in other ways as well, including curriculum development and the provision of work experience. One of the public utility company personnel had already by that time visited the CTC to talk to pupils and attend policy meetings.

It is much easier for a manager or personnel officer to know that their company had been approached by the CTC for help than that it has not. Such letters do not always reach the most appropriate people to deal with them; it is possible that approaches had been made at senior level but had not filtered down to local management. Eighteen of the representatives of organizations within the two samples combined stated that they were not aware that their company had been asked to support the CTC. Some of these companies were very large, and the person interviewed expressed puzzlement that no such invitation had been made. Indeed, several felt that their company might be a useful supporter, and that, at the very least, an approach by the CTC would have been a valuable public relations exercise raising awareness among potential employers.

Amongst the representatives of the companies interviewed within the travel-to-work area there was a high level of support for the CTC concept and for the presence of a local CTC. Not unexpectedly the most favourable opinions tended to come from those most dissatisfied with the present maintained educational system. Comments ranged from 'sound' to 'brilliant', although most also expressed some reservations as the college was, as yet, unproven. Several of those interviewed also recognized that other schools might suffer by not having the resources or industrial support that the CTC had; one respondent said that similar facilities should be available in all schools.

In the wider sample of Birmingham and Solihull organizations drawn from the Chamber of Commerce, the most evident characteristic was lack of knowledge about the CTC. No official contact had been reported with most of the companies and the information held by the respondents resulted from personal interest and newspaper, radio and television coverage. The media coverage seems to have been a more important general source of information than material from the CTC itself. Moreover, on several occasions the interviewer found himself having to offer an explanation of the CTC concept. Nevertheless, the manufacturing concerns tended to view the CTC idea more favourably than service organizations, primarily because they saw the possibility of the CTC providing some of their future recruitment needs. Some of the latter felt that they would probably get involved with the CTC, but only on the same basis as any other school in the area. In general, these organizations were more qualified in their support, emphasizing their competitive position and the lack of spare money to support such ventures. Apart from Lucas Industries, who are one of the founder sponsors, there was little confidence amongst this group of managers that the CTC would have any positive effect on the quality of other schools. Indeed, some of those interviewed expressed concern about the selection methods that might be used by the CTC. One personnel director of a large manufacturing company, for example, feared that the CTC would become like a grammar school. He argued that it would have very little impact on his company if this turned out to be the case.

The most well-argued case for supporting the CTC was put forward by a senior executive from Lucas Industries, who was first interviewed in early 1988. He claimed that Lucas had been interested in education and training for many years, and that this had originally stemmed from a realization that there was a lack of engineers to recruit. He argued that the educational system was not providing what industry needed and that there was a strong anti-industry attitude in schools which needed to be changed. Education, he argued, should be more like industry and respond quickly and flexibly to changes in the market. There needed to be changes in the management of education and far more innovation and diversity.

Lucas had been involved with local TVEI from the initial consultations with the Manpower Services Commission (now the Training Agency) onwards. The company had supported that initiative and the CTC not because it expected to get anything directly in return for its investment, but because it saw both as important moves towards a more responsive educational system. Change from the top down was seen as largely unsuccessful and too brutal, while change from the bottom up was seen as having the advantage of being democratic but the major problem of being too slow. The executive compared the sixteen years taken to introduce GCSE through democratic means from the bottom up, with the far faster change that was occurring through 'sideways' initiatives such as TVEI and CTCs. Here, funding was made available on a lavish, though experimental, basis for those who wished to take part and to act quickly. He emphasized that it was not that the company emphatically believed in the CTC idea as such or did not believe in it, for that matter, but that it saw this type of initiative as a model for the introduction of change and a move towards a more responsive educational system. He argued

> the CTC is an experiment and, at the end of five or seven years it's time to take stock and say 'What has the CTC movement achieved? What have been its successes? What have been its failures? . . . And what about replication?' It may be that the CTCs cannot be replicated if they are successful, and they may stay as an interesting and separate form of education.

He felt that it was likely that parts of the CTC would be successful and parts not successful, but that the general effect was still likely to be an improvement in performance in education and that the experiment would show better ways of managing education.

The company was one of the few that had responded positively to the idea of sponsoring a CTC as a result of the original DES booklet in 1986. Although an election was imminent and it was recognized that the CTC idea was politically sensitive, it rapidly decided to conduct a feasibility study to assess the extent of industrial support for a local CTC. In the event, they were overtaken by events. Hanson plc stepped in with its major donation, and the study was never conducted. However, Lucas still played a major role in bringing together an industrial team from companies which had shown some sort of interest – financial, practical, advisory or just some vague interest – to help to establish the new college. Lucas has continued its close involvement with the CTC through secondment of executives, acting as advisers and providing funding.

It would appear that Kenneth Baker's statement that

> the unique thing about the CTC is that it involves industrial-
> ists at an early stage in a more committed and involved way
> than is the way they generally get involved
>
> (*Panorama*, 'A Class Apart' BBC TV 1988)

is partially true in the Kingshurst case. There, not only has there
been substantial financial commitment from industrialists, but also
there has been time and expertise of senior executives devoted to
the development of the CTC. However, the responses from this
small sample of local employers do not fit neatly into any patterns.
There was a range from high levels of support to ignorance, with
the majority of those interviewed expressing some general support,
but with specific reservations. Although the sample is too small and
non-representative for clear generalizations to be made, it does
allow the myths of wholesale support or opposition to the CTC
concept by industry to be rejected. The reality is more complicated
than this, with various industries responding in an individual and
sometimes idiosyncratic way to the CTC initiative.

8

Conclusion

Developments in the national CTC plan

Even though Sir Cyril Taylor announced in December 1989 that private funding had been secured for all twenty of the proposed CTCs, it now seems unlikely that the total will ever reach that number. Kingshurst, which opened in 1988, had been followed by Djanogly in Nottingham and Macmillan in Middlesbrough in 1989, and another four in 1990. Eight more were expected in 1991, and there were a couple of less definite possibilities. These are listed below:

Name	Main sponsor	Opening date
Kingshurst CTC, Solihull	Hanson plc	Sept. 1988
Djanogly College, Nottingham	Harry Djanogly	Sept. 1989
Macmillan College, Middlesbrough	BAT Industries	Sept. 1989
Bradford CTC	Dixons plc	Sept. 1990
Emmanuel College, Gateshead	Reg Vardy	Sept. 1990
Leigh CTC, Dartford	Geoffrey Leigh	Sept. 1990
Harris CTC, Croydon	Harris Charitable Trust	Sept. 1990
Telford CTC	Mercer's Foundation	Sept. 1991
Lewisham CTC	Haberdashers' Aske's Charitable Trust	Sept. 1991
Bacon's CTC, Bermondsey	Southwark Diocesan Church of England Board of Education	Sept. 1991

Name	Main sponsor	Opening date
Corby CTC	Hugh de Capell Brooke	Sept. 1991
Derby	Landau Foundation	Sept. 1991
Glasgow CTC	Trusthouse Forte	Sept. 1991
CCTA, Selhurst, Croydon	British Record Industry Trust	Sept. 1991
Wandsworth CTC	ADT Group plc	Sept. 1991
Swindon CTC	W.H. Smith	not known
(unsited)	Wolfson Foundation	not known

While City Technology Colleges had been introduced, in part, to extend the range of choice available to parents and pupils, the failure to find sufficient sites and sponsors for the original proposals has led to a far wider range of CTCs than could ever have been envisaged. The original idea of lavishly redeveloping redundant buildings or of custom building colleges on 'green-field' sites has now been abandoned as too expensive, and various other ways of establishing CTCs have gradually developed.

The CTC which opened in Gateshead in September 1990 is a good example of this unplanned diversity. Its sponsors are an influential group of evangelical Christians who let it be known in late 1988 that about £1.5 million could be found for a specifically Christian CTC. It would seem that there were informal links between this group and those on the New Right who pushed for changes to the 1988 Education Reform Act on religious education and assemblies (see for example Burn and Hart 1988). The proposal also linked to the work of Caroline Cox and others who had been campaigning for government support for small Christian schools (Walford 1991b). The main donors were Mr Peter Vardy, who is a member of the Free Evangelical/Christian Brethren Church and chairman of Reg Vardy Motor Group, and Mr Albert Dicken, chairman of a home-improvement chain, Dickens Ltd. Originally there were no plans that CTCs should be linked to particular faiths, and DES guidelines make it clear that admission to a CTC should not be subject to any denominational test. However, while the Gateshead CTC is open to children of all denominations and faiths, it has a distinctive emphasis on a specific form of Christian ethics and values. Staff are expected to be 'firmly committed to the aims of the college'. The cost to the government is expected to be about £6.9 million. Apart from the controversy generated over whether CTCs should have a specific religious link, Gateshead also came under fire for the site chosen as it was not an inner-city site, but was on the edge of the countryside. It was argued by opposers that the CTC was a very long way from any inner-city working-class pupils of the sort originally intended for CTCs.

One of the most controversial developments was the idea of making some voluntary aided schools, previously an integral part of the maintained sector, into CTCs. This was a possibility because, although the voluntary aided schools are heavily funded by the LEAs, they are under the control of external organizations, usually the Roman Catholic Church or the Church of England. There are also some voluntary aided schools which were founded, sometimes several centuries ago, by specific charities and companies, and some of these schools' governors have been persuaded that it would be advantageous for the schools to become CTCs.

Two such voluntary aided schools were the Haberdashers' Aske's Boys' and Girls' Schools in Lewisham, South London, which were founded in the last century. There was a long legal battle involving eight ILEA-appointed Labour governors and a group of company, Conservative and parent governors over plans to close the existing schools and re-establish them as CTCs. Further problems occurred as parents of the girls' school voted against the proposed change while parents of the boys' school voted in favour. The overall vote was 57 per cent in favour. Eventually the sponsoring company, Haberdashers', provided the existing site, buildings and about £1 million of new money over five years, while the government provided £4 million for refurbishment and equipment for the new role.

Similar wrangling was initiated by a plan for London's Docklands. Here an existing Church of England voluntary aided school, Bacon's, is to close and the site sold. The money raised and the school's foundation income will then go towards a Bacon's CTC in Docklands on land given by the London Docklands Development Corporation for the school. The Philip and Pauline Harris Charitable Trust is expected to put in another £1 million. The interest here is that Bacon's had been trying to move from its cramped and split site for many years and had found a new site in Surrey Docks. The government had refused to find the necessary capital expenditure, but indicated that it would help if the school relocated as a CTC. Parents of children at the school had voted two to one against the scheme, but it is still going ahead.

The two CTCs in Dartford, Kent, and in Croydon marked a further distinct change in the national policy for the colleges. Both

of these CTCs are 'conversions' of existing LEA schools. Both
Kent County Council and Croydon Metropolitan Borough
Council are Conservative controlled and have co-operated with
the City Technology Colleges Trust to expand the original CTC
concept to include the 'upgrading' of existing schools. At Dartford,
the existing 11–18 Downs School was closed and reopened as The
Leigh City Technology College. Staff were reported to be against
the proposal, stressing that the school was already thriving, well
equipped and in better buildings than others in the neighbourhood
(Heron 1989). Nevertheless, a few of the staff from The Downs
School have been appointed to the new college. This includes the
school's Deputy Head, who has become the new Principal. The
college agreed to take on all 800 of the existing pupils from The
Downs School as long as the pupils fully accepted the college's
rules and principles, including a commitment to remain in education or training until 18 and to complete homework assignments.
Most significantly, the CTC is also committed to continue to take
all children whose parents live in the areas which were formerly
served by The Downs School, subject only to their acceptance of
these same college rules and principles. This implies a more limited
form of selection for those children living close to the college. In
addition the CTC continues to house an integral Hearing Impaired
Unit for the area, whose pupils will have automatic right of entry.
Kent County Council received £3 million of the total of £7
million capital budget for the college for the lease of the building
and grounds. Mr Geoffrey Leigh and the Wellcome Foundation
provided about £1.5 million, with the government providing the
remainder. An interesting feature here is that the Wellcome
Foundation funding is designed to support community provision
for education and recreation for adults in the area, and thus is not
technically part of the CTC which, by law, can provide only for
students below the age of 19.

In Croydon, the existing 11–16 Sylvan High School belonging to Croydon Council closed in August 1990 and immediately
reopened as the Harris City Technology College. The main sponsorship is from the Philip and Pauline Harris Charitable Trust,
established by Sir Philip Harris and his wife while he was chairman
of Harris Queensway, and from David Lewes. Together they have
contributed some £1.5 million, with the government providing an
additional £6 million. Croydon Borough Council's support for
the scheme was not pure altruism, for it was paid £4 million of this

total in return for the lease of the land and buildings. There was
fierce opposition from governors to the proposals (Conniff 1989).
Parents were given no official right to vote on the change, but
some 97 per cent of the 55 per cent of parents who voted in an
unofficial ballot, voted to keep the school as an 11–16 high school.
Their voices went unheard. Following a particular interest of the
main sponsor, the new CTC was to have a special unit for dyslexic
children. The CTC will also take over an existing leisure centre on
the site which were previously run by the parks and Recreation
Division of the Council. This will be developed and continued to
provide facilities for the local community. As with the Leigh CTC,
it is unclear how this community involvement can be an integral
part of the CTC, which by law caters for students below the age of
19.

Croydon is also the site of the first City College for the
Technology of the Arts (CCTA), the London School for the Performing Arts, supported by Richard Branson's Virgin Group and
others. Here, part of the site of Croydon College, which caters for
16–18 year olds, was acquired. In addition to longer hours of
working each day, the college is to have a four-term year, with no
long summer holiday, and may eventually have boarding accommodation. Unlike other CTCs, it will take children only from ages
13 to 18, and its catchment area extends to all of London. It is of
note that when the college was officially launched, it was stated
that the idea of establishing a School for the Performing Arts had
been first mooted some six years earlier – way before the CTC idea
– and was linked to Performing Arts Schools in the USA, which
had received great attention through the television programme
Fame (Hadfield 1989). Support for the CCTA has wavered during
the planning process, leading to the postponement of the opening
date by a year.

The establishment of a network of CTCs has been fraught
with false starts and controversy, but one of the most unlikely
failures occurred after September 1989 when a college to be based
on the educational ideas of Rudolf Steiner was announced for
Brighton. Brighton already has a private Rudolf Steiner school
with about 200 pupils, which is part of a group of such schools in
Britain and abroad. The planned CTC was to have no official links
with the private school, but the Project Team for the CTC included an ex-teacher from the school (Makins 1989). The main
sponsor was to be Greenleaf Planters, a local interior landscaping

company – which caused some commentators to call this a 'green CTC'. However, by May 1990, what had been announced as a firm plan had been abandoned amid police investigations of illegal commissions on land, and inability of the sponsors to find sufficient funding.

In October 1989 the new Secretary of State for Education, John MacGregor, confirmed that the Treasury was not prepared to go beyond the originally planned twenty CTCs. With costs at that point of £44 million from industry and £135 million from the Treasury, Sir Cyril Taylor admitted that the capital cost of buying sites or carrying out refurbishments was proving too high, and that any further CTCs would have to be funded jointly with LEAs. If CTCs could be established with the co-operation of LEAs, and thus without the need to pay for the original school buildings, there would be major savings. He hoped that the revised concept could be extended into all LEAs. This new plan would broaden the range of CTCs far beyond that of inner-city urban areas. The first of this new type of CTC may occur at Wandsworth, where the new LEA wishes to establish one fully independent CTC and another owned by the LEA within a fully 'magnetized' system. Some further indication of this greater degree of co-operation with LEAs was evident in June 1990 when the Secretary of State announced that he would consult parents and councils on future CTCs and on those proposed for Derby, Telford and Wandsworth. However, any short-lived optimism was quickly crushed as heavy criticism of all three plans was swiftly overruled.

A provisional evaluation of The CTC Kingshurst

City Technology Colleges are intensely ideological. The original concept was born in controversy and the colleges have remained at the centre of dispute. The preceding chapters of this book have presented a case study of the first of these colleges to be opened at Kingshurst, Solihull. One of the main aims of the book is simply to describe the nature of that first college within its local environment, and to try to assess the extent to which criticisms of the CTC plan have been justified for this first college. This section brings together some of the previous discussion about the case study and attempts to assess the effects of The CTC Kingshurst on the local educational environment. While accepting the limitations of the case study, and that all CTCs will differ significantly from each other, the chapter then discusses the implications of the study's findings in the national context.

The conclusions are not simple. The previous section has shown that the national plan announced in 1986 has changed considerably since that time. It has been adjusted to adapt to the lack of support given to the idea by industry and commerce, to the difficulty of finding suitable sites within largely Labour-controlled urban areas, and to the realities of building new schools from scratch in a hostile environment. These changes have led to a confusion of aims and objectives for the colleges, which means that criteria for the success of the innovation are not clear. Further, the changes have meant that the decisions made by Kingshurst in the early stages of its life would not necessarily be the decisions that would be made now. The college has had to adapt within the changing environment in which it has found itself.

Chapters 3–6 were based upon a period of fieldwork conducted in the CTC during the autumn term of 1989. They present an account of various aspects of life in the CTC when there were only two years of students. It is far too early to evaluate the long-term effectiveness of anything that college has chosen to do; however, it is possible to discuss short-term effects.

In 1987 the Association of Metropolitan Authorities was particularly concerned that CTCs might exacerbate staffing difficulties in shortage subjects, by using increased salary levels to attract a disproportionate number of well-qualified teachers in science, mathematics, craft, design and technology, computing and similar areas. It was expected that local extreme shortages in these subjects might occur as a result of teachers from the area being attracted to the CTC from local schools. The evidence presented in Chapter 3 indicated that such fears had not materialized. The vast majority of teachers appointed at the time of the research had come from the state sector, but they had been drawn from a wide geographical area. The local area had not suffered a loss of skilled teachers, and there appears to have been a movement of such skilled teachers from socially more middle-class areas to this predominantly working-class area. Furthermore, most of the teachers appointed to the CTC had not had significant previous experience of information technology, and the majority have become skilled since their appointment. The CTC has thus led to a net increase in the number of computer-literate teachers in the whole system. While this is a welcome outcome, it is worth noting that it would obviously have been possible to have achieved this particular objective at far lower cost through alternative means. There is more doubt about the effect of the CTC on technical support staff, who have in the main been drawn from the local area. In addition, the private school status of the college has enabled it to appoint staff on salaries and conditions of service different from that imposed nationally. The salary structure has some significant features to which most teachers' unions would strongly object. In addition, the college day and term are longer than in LEA schools, and much is expected of teachers. It might be argued that the acceptance of these different salary scales and conditions of working by teachers in a school largely supported by the state has made it easier for government to introduce local pay and conditions bargaining for LEA schools.

Chapter 4 showed that, while the college is well supplied with facilities in most areas, the resources available are not as generous as some critics suppose. Indeed, the college is under-resourced in some areas. The staff have developed a broad curriculum which includes more information technology throughout the curriculum than is possible in most other schools, but have largely drawn upon what they consider to be 'good practice' in state schools in constructing their curriculum. For the most part, the curriculum of the CTC does not differ greatly from that in many state schools. Curriculum development is still at an early stage, and for young children but, as yet, the direct involvement of industrialists in the development of specific curriculum components has not been as close as in some of the LEA comprehensive schools in its catchment area. Such close contact is unlikely in the first few years of the college simply because, no matter how hard working the staff are, the effort involved in establishing a new school from scratch simply allows insufficient time. The direct involvement of industrialists in developing curricular for BTEC and International Baccalaureate courses is also initially unlikely to be significant, due to lack of time. In under a year, alongside everyday teaching, administration and pastoral work, the CTC's small staff have had to develop new courses for BTEC First Diplomas in five subjects, BTEC National in twelve subjects, the Kingshurst Diploma and the International Baccalaureate (practically all the staff had no previous experience of any of these), as well as a whole new third year scheme of work.

The Kingshurst curriculum gives great emphasis to collaborative group work, decision-making, and building self-confidence. The college makes considerable demands on the students and, in return, is prepared to grant them more autonomy than is common in LEA schools. The college provides a structured and supportive environment in which to learn. Overall, relationships between staff and students are very positive, and the vast majority of students are highly enthusiastic about the college. There is an infectious excitement throughout the staff and students, and it is difficult to believe that attendance at the CTC is not a highly positive experience for the vast majority of children selected. Both staff and students recognize that they are part of a very 'special' school and work to ensure that the experiment is successful.

Any evaluation of an innovation in education faces the difficulty of Hawthorne effects (Mayo 1983), whereby the very fact that there is a change in curriculum, teaching method or whatever, makes those involved in the innovation feel special. This feeling of being out of the ordinary makes it more likely that the results of the innovation will be successful, yet success may be more related to the fact that there has been any change than to the content of the actual change made. At Kingshurst CTC, being 'special' is almost a way of life. Both teachers and students are continually reminded of their privileged status through television, radio and newspaper reports; through visits from politicians, educationists, industrialists and even Prince Philip; and through constant reminders within the CTC itself that they are part of something different and that something extraordinary is expected of them. All good schools try to make their pupils feel special, but the CTC has a head start on practically all LEA schools. In sum, unless something goes dramatically wrong, it is difficult to believe that these students will not greatly benefit from being at the CTC – socially and in terms of educational qualifications and occupational success.

The question of selection

Selection of students is an important first part of making children feel 'special'. Chapter 6 showed that The City Technology College, Kingshurst, is a selective school. More children apply to attend the college than it is allowed by the DES to accommodate, so it has to select which applicants are to be given places. The method that the CTC uses was described in Chapter 6 and is designed to obtain a spread of different abilities from amongst those who apply. The spread of abilities is not representative of the abilities of all the children in the catchment area, but is broadly representative in terms of the abilities of the children who apply. However, the nature of the process of application and interviewing of parents and children means that the children who apply and are selected are likely to be from amongst the group of well-motivated parents who are aware of the importance of education. Selection is in part based on motivation. For those students living some distance from the College and those few students selected from outside the catchment area, selection is also on the ability and willingness to pay for transport to the school.

Many critics claim that selection automatically means that the CTC cannot be a comprehensive school. However, it is worth remembering that all popular schools are forced to be selective in some way. The moves to open enrolment within the 1988 Education Reform Act do not change the fact that, if more children apply than there are places available, the school is forced to select. In most cases the main criterion used is nearness of the home to the school – those who are nearer to the school in question are likely to have a higher chance of obtaining a place than those who live further away. In practice this means that selection for popular 'comprehensive' schools is often an ability to pay – to pay for a house near to a particular school which is perceived to be good.

A good example of this was seen when Solihull tried to re-introduce selective education in 1983. The main opposition to the idea came from middle-class parents who had bought homes in the catchment areas of perceived good schools. Estate agents made it clear that the cost of their homes included a cost associated with being in 'good' catchment areas. These parents objected to the proposed change to selective education, because it meant that their children's education became more uncertain. A less able child might just not be selected and be forced to attend a less popular school. Many of the families in north Solihull would very much like to live in south Solihull. It is a far more pleasant area, and the schools are generally perceived to be 'better'. They are unable to do so, simply because they cannot afford the high costs of housing. Even after open enrolment, public transport to south Solihull is both time consuming and expensive, for the LEA does not pay transport costs other than to the nearest (or, where appropriate, Roman Catholic) school; free choice is limited by financial considerations (see Ashworth *et al.* 1988). This is far from exceptional, for the majority of popular 'comprehensive' schools throughout the country actually select on ability to pay for nearby housing, yet this does not appear to have been recognized by many critics of selection.

There is also a major irony in Birmingham City Council's attitude towards the CTC on its doorstep. It runs a highly academically selective system where about 9 per cent of children are given places. The odds are stacked such that it is far more difficult for a girl to obtain a place than a boy. Parents apply on behalf of their children to take an entrance test at one of the grammar schools. Thus, in exactly the same way as for the CTC, selection depends on the motivation of parents. It also depends on ability and willingness to pay, for travel expenses are not provided by the LEA in most cases, even though the travel distance may be well over three miles. Under the most restrictive definition, Kingshurst CTC may not be a comprehensive school but, as Stephen Ball (1988) and others have now recognized, the so-called comprehensive reform never really happened. The real change that occurred after the 1960s was a concealment of the divisions and inequalities in education, rendering them more complex and less visible.

Nevertheless, apart from the wider social issues, the visible selection process used by the CTC and by Birmingham LEA has both positive and negative effects on the individual children involved. Those who are offered a place have the personal satisfaction of having been selected in preference to others, but those who are rejected suffer from this early evaluation of their unsuitability. We do not know the relative forces of these two sides to the equation.

Effects of The CTC Kingshurst on other schools

One of the models used by the CTC for its possible wider role is that of a catalyst for change within education. It does not see itself as being just another school, but as being one that can influence the practice of education elsewhere. In contrast, it was shown in Chapter 7 that local schools perceived the CTC's main effect on them as being the removal of highly motivated potential pupils and, not surprisingly, they did not see this as a positive influence.

The local LEA comprehensive schools did not see the CTC as having any positive influence on their curriculum at all. To varying degrees, all of the schools had been involved with industry and commerce before the CTC started, and saw their various BTEC, technological and vocational courses as natural developments from earlier work. TVEI was seen as particularly important within those schools that had taken part. Some of the schools had been highly involved in innovative work on education, technology and industry and were themselves acting as catalysts for change in the other nearby LEA schools by working with them on new projects. The essence of a catalyst in scientific terms is that a reaction is poised to proceed, or is proceeding very slowly, but that the catalyst acts to speed up the change by making contact with those involved. Catalysts only work by being in contact with others, but this was exactly what the CTC was unable to do through shortage of time and personnel, and from the way in which it was established in conflict with local LEA schools. Where the CTC did have an effect on staff in other schools it was to lower their level of morale. Teachers at the LEA comprehensive schools resented the criticism of their own schools and of themselves that the presence of a CTC implied, and felt that competition between their under-funded schools and the well-resourced CTC was fundamentally unfair.

One area where the CTC did have an effect was with the marketing of the LEA schools. Both the east Birmingham and north Solihull groups of secondary schools had produced and circulated new advertising to the parents in the local neighbourhood, and had increased their concern with projecting a positive image in the media. Most of the schools now had someone with specific responsibility for promoting the school in the area. However, the joint efforts lasted for only one year, and all of the schools argue that even without the CTC there would have been major changes in marketing of their schools as a result of the 1988 Education Reform Act.

The effect of the CTC and the increased marketing of all schools may have had the additional effect of raising interest in education and schools amongst local parents and children. Education has also been given a higher priority by local politicians and increased interest may have been generated amongst managers of local industry and commerce. It is likely that the presence of the CTC, with its associated national media attention, has generated a greater local interest than the changes in the 1988 Education Reform Act would have done by themselves.

CTCs as ideology in action

The establishment of CTCs, and The CTC Kingshurst in particular, can be seen as an example of ideology in action. In this section
we shall attempt to unravel the different strands of the ideological
skein on which the CTC concept is suspended. We relate this
discussion to some of the real and perceived problems of the British
political economy and the relation between education and industry, and consider the extent to which the CTC initiative engages in
a meaningful way with these problems. For ease of presentation
and analysis we have located four major strands, but in reality these
strands interweave in complex ways. The concept of ideology used
here was developed in classical terms by Marx and Engels (1939)
and Mannheim (1960) and modified by such authors as Merton
(1968), Giddens (1985) and Perkin (1989).

The first major strand that the CTC concept draws upon is
the perceived need to do something about the education of those
living in the deprived inner city. There are various threads to this
strand. One implication is that existing provision, run mainly by
Labour-controlled LEAs and stereotyped as the 'looney left', was
failing to meet the legitimate aspirations of pupils and parents living
in the inner city. Instead, they were seen as providing an irrelevant
or even subversive curriculum where peace education, multi-
cultural and sex education were given prominence over 'real' education. A further thread in this strand was Margaret Thatcher's
personal mission to extirpate the basis of socialism in the cities. Nor
should it be forgotten that one of the most dramatic confrontations
with Thatcherite policy was the inner-city riots of the early 1980s.
Here it was thought that the complex problems of unemployment,
racial violence, antagonism to the police and general dissolution of
social norms might be remedied through appropriate schooling.

The second major strand, again composed of many threads,
concerns the links between education, technology and industry.
Here the aim is to fit pupils better into employment, and is a
response to the mass youth unemployment of the early 1980s, and
a more recent realization of growing skills shortages. Another
thread is the positive emphasis on technology as part of the school
curriculum which needs to be enhanced to meet the needs of the
economy. Lastly, there is also seen to be a need for industry to
become involved with education through funding, and to overcome the perceived 'anti-industry' spirit within education by

promoting within schools an ethos more in tune with enterprise, wealth creation and good management.

The third strand in the complex ideology supporting the CTCs is the emphasis on choice, diversity and inequality of provision. The argument here is that choice is increased by providing a new form of private school outside the LEA sector, but charging no fees. Parents and children with particular technological interests and aspirations are able to choose a school with this emphasis. A rather understated thread to this strand is the necessary corollary of selection for the schools if they prove popular.

The fourth of these interlinked strands is that of being anti-public sector provision and pro-private sector and privatization. In some ways this is the most obviously political and ideological resonance of the CTC concept – the attacks on LEAs and glorification of the private sector were what those at the Conservative Party Annual Conference in 1986 responded to most enthusiastically when the CTCs were announced.

These four strands are the crucial ones in the ideological support for CTCs. The range of different colours to these strands is important. Some are clearly political, others educational and yet others social. The result is that they can elicit identification from a range of different constituencies, such that Thatcherite militants, concerned industrialists and progressive educators can all be brought into an uneasy alliance. The strength of the overall ideology supporting CTCs is that it identifies real and perceived problems within our society and appears to deal with them. What are these problems? Do CTCs actually deal with them?

The real and perceived problems that CTCs appear to deal with can be again discussed through our four interlinked strands. First, the set of problems bracketed by the phrase 'inner city'. Within many inner-city areas there is certainly urban decay and squalor in terms of housing, schools and health services. There are high levels of unemployment, racial tension, high crime rates, high insurance rates, and a set of conditions which induces feelings of alienation and anger. The schools are often old and in a bad state of repair, while truancy, violence and apathy are common amongst pupils. There is an important and complex argument about the relative importance of economic, political and cultural factors in creating the phenomenon of the 'inner city', which itself has contours which go well beyond the geographical definition. However, few would contest the importance of the failure of material investment (both public and private) as being a crucial causal factor and characteristic of the problem. The more contentious questions are centred on the political and social conditions which might bring about that necessary investment and the necessary empowerment of the inhabitants of the inner city. Can these be manipulated from outside? What role does education play? Would a CTC be a catalyst to solve these problems or a diversion?

The second strand is the industry, education and technology nexus. Such attempts to link the education system more closely to the perceived needs of industry for a well-skilled, motivated and disciplined workforce are far from new (Pollard *et al.* 1988). Although the argument has ebbed and flowed over time, Reeder (1979) has shown that criticism from industrialists about schooling has intensified at times of economic under-performance and decline, as industry searches for a scapegoat for its own failures. It was thus to be expected that such arguments should gain prominence in the early 1980s. None the less, international comparisons of investment in training by government and by industry and of staying-on rates beyond school leaving age make it clear that Britain has real problems in this area. Technical education has continued to take second place to the academic curriculum, and Wiener (1981), Perkin (1989) and many others have variously analysed the failure of English polity, economy and society to recognize the importance of industry, technical training and education for competition in the contemporary world economy. The low and declining levels of first-choice applicants to British universities in engineering (dropping from 20,000 in 1981 to 13,000 in 1988), and in computing (down 8 per cent in the same time from an already low 5,000), together with a halving of the number of craft and technician trainees achieving a certificate of basic training from 1981 to 1989 illustrate the seriousness of the problem at all levels.

The third strand of ideas within the ideology supporting the CTCs is that of choice and diversity of provision, with the possibility of associated selection procedures to allocate children to their most 'appropriate' schools. Again, questions of diversity of provision and selection have a long and intractable history. The results were seen at their clearest in the period shortly after the Second World War when some LEAs had a tripartite system of grammar, secondary technical and secondary modern schools alongside a further diversity of private schools. Advocates of such a system see this diversity of provision and choice as leading to the most efficient and effective use of resources, and to all children being taught in a way that best befits them. Those who are most suited to high-level technical education are well provided for, as are those who would benefit from a traditional academic education. Children are seen as differing in their interests and motivations, such that it is best for all concerned to separate them to receive different types of education.

The fourth set of problems to which the CTC ideology addresses itself is that of the balance between public and private provision. Under this strand of the ideology the public sector is characterized as bureaucratic, unaccountable and essentially parasitic and out of touch with wealth-creating industry, while the private sector is seen as flexible, efficient, dynamic and responsive to the needs of the consumer and therefore the community. It is undoubtedly true that the worst of the LEAs are bureaucratic and wasteful. Many Heads have tales to tell of how long they have waited for a broken window to be mended, or for more stationery to arrive. But there is great variation, with the best LEAs providing the benefits of economies of scale, overall planning for the needs of the area, essential back-up for Heads and other teachers, realistic in-service provision, curriculum development advice, and more. A similar variability is to be found in the private sector of education, where the major schools offer privilege (Walford 1990a), but the worst schools provide poor teaching in drab and unstimulating environments (Walford 1991c). A more realistic picture might recognize the deficiencies, strengths and weaknesses of both sectors.

We have outlined four interwoven strands within the ideology used to justify and promote the establishment of CTC, and related them to the problem area with which they deal. The next important step in our investigation is to assess the extent to which the CTCs actually address these areas or divert attention and understanding away from the underlying problems.

Taking first the set of problems associated with the inner city, it is unlikely that the CTCs will be central to any solution. The inner-city areas are predominantly Labour controlled, and those councils, reacting to the advocacy of the CTCs as anti-public sector and the attack on their own schools, have unsurprisingly refused sites and co-operation. So far, CTCs have thus not been placed in the key inner-city areas. The target area in Birmingham was Handsworth, scene of inner-city riots in the early 1980s, but Kingshurst CTC in north Solihull has turned out to be the nearest possible site. We have recognized, however, that areas of deprivation are not limited to the geographical inner city, and that Kingshurst's catchment area contains many people suffering from various forms of deprivation. Nevertheless, the problems of the inner city are deeply rooted in a failure of public and private investment, and lack of political and economic power of the residents. We predict that those predominantly working-class pupils who have been selected for Kingshurst CTC will receive an education that will increase their personal power and confidence. It will also probably increase their chances of higher education and high-status employment but this, ironically, will mean leaving their home environment. Success for these pupils will probably mean leaving the area in which they were born rather than fighting to change it. The much-quoted dictum of Basil Bernstein (1970) that 'education cannot compensate for society' still holds true. Schools may mitigate the effects of society but, unless initiatives are co-ordinated with sufficient structural changes involving substantially increased public and private investment in the inner city, improved education in one school may simply lead to the flight of the beneficiaries.

The CTC Kingshurst is isolated from its local environment. There is little local consultation or co-operation. Parents, local community leaders or local councillors are not present on the governing body, and do not play any significant part in the running of the college. Apart from the links with business, contact with the community is as consumers of a product, and there is no space for local influence or control. It is difficult to see how the CTC can help empower local citizens and be a force for change within the local area, except at one remove through their children.

Similar difficulties are evident when we examine the set of problems associated with education, industry and technology. We have already documented in earlier chapters the limited support from major corporations for the CTC concept. For some of these organizations this probably reflects a fundamental lack of interest in education and training which is unlikely to be dispersed by a scatter of CTCs and exhortations by Conservative politicians to back them with funds and resources. For many, however, this is a reasonable and realistic reluctance to back a rather idiosyncratic experiment when they are already committed to a range of schemes linking and funding technology and industry in LEA schools.

TVEI has been very successful in many schools, and industry and commerce is acting very sensibly if it continues to promote and develop a range of links with many schools rather than concentrate them expensively in one.

Within Kingshurst there is a much wider range of technology than available in most LEA schools, and we confidently predict that students will use this equipment across the curriculum in ways which will build their competence in information technology. However, of itself, this does not mean that a high profile is being given to scientific and technological education and training. The post-16 provision, for example, is to be geared to BTEC and International Baccalaureate (IB) qualifications, and the inclusion of BTEC at school level is recognition of the importance of technical education. Yet it is expected that up to 50 per cent will take IB. We predict that it will be the more able student who will take the IB and that this will lead to a hierarchy of courses within the college with the far more academic IB having higher status over the technological BTECs.

McCulloch (1989: 182) sums up the problem of the promotion of technical education towards the end of his historical study of the secondary technical schools established after the Second World War.

> the question of whether to attempt to influence existing, established institutions or to develop new rival structures. The experience of the secondary technical schools graphically demonstrates both the attractions and the pitfalls of the second approach. On the one hand it promised novelty and fewer constraints, although in practice the schools could not escape the influence of established traditions and values. On the other it meant confinement to a small and effectively marginal group of schools with relatively few pupils. On this evidence there are important advantages to be found in a policy of 'integration', such as TVEI, as opposed to one of 'independence' such as the secondary technical schools and the CTCs.

If we listen to the lessons from history, it would seem that the idea of new, separate schools for technology is more likely to marginalize that activity rather than encourage it in the vast majority of other schools. The existence of such colleges allows the major private schools and the grammar schools to retain their existing roles of providing an academic curriculum for the most able pupils.

Given that the CTCs will not be able to challenge the existing hierarchy of schools by themselves, if they accept their role as centres of excellence for technology, they will find themselves some distance from the top of any hierarchy. If they wish to move upwards, they will have to deviate from this role – as Kingshurst already appears to be doing.

This idea of a hierarchy of schools directly links to the third of the strands within the ideology supporting CTCs – choice and diversity of schools. We have seen that the overt concern here is with efficiency and with providing appropriate education according to ability and need. However, in Britain diversity of schools and inequality of provision has long been associated with social class and gender, and there is little reason to suppose that this new diversity will operate in any different way. The comprehensive ideal attempted to overcome some of these difficulties, and to provide a socially mixed educational environment. In contrast, the CTCs have played a major part in re-legitimizing inequality of provision for different pupils, and selection of children according to interests and motivation. The CTC concept was rapidly followed by the idea of grant-maintained schools and locally managed schools all competing for pupils in a market. The inevitable result is a hierarchy of schools with the private sector at the head (with some pupils on Assisted Places), the CTCs and grant-maintained schools next, and the various locally managed LEA schools following.

The idea of increased choice within this diversity is as attractive as it is unrealistic. While there are falling school rolls, parental choices can be used to decide which LEA schools will close, but once this has occurred there will be less choice rather than more, and the choices will all be between over-crowded schools. Just as with The CTC Kingshurst, once there are more applicants than places, the more popular schools will become selective, and those children not selected will be forced to attend schools which were not of their choosing. The problem is that this process of selection is unlikely to be random, but is likely to follow the lead of the CTCs and depend on the motivation and knowledge of parents and children, and the ability of both to present themselves well to selectors (Walford 1990b). Without being condescending to the many working-class and ethnic minority parents who continue to fight against the odds to achieve a good education for their children, on average such parents are likely to be less knowledgeable about their children's education than middle-class parents. They are more likely to have had a poorer education themselves, with little experience of further or higher education, and are less likely to be able to negotiate educational bureaucracies or present themselves as 'supportive' parents in interview with Headteachers or others. While it is possible that some selectors will actively discriminate in favour of under-privileged groups, given the strength and durability of the British class system and ethnic differences, greater diversity of schools is likely to reinforce rather than reduce class and ethnic differences.

This leads directly to the fourth strand in the ideology supporting the CTCs – the support for private education and privatization of education. Protagonists such as Stuart Sexton (1987) have made no secret of their desire for a fully privatized educational system, where there is a direct financial relationship between the provider and the 'consumer' (Walford 1990a). Many of the ideas contained within Sexton's 'Radical Policy' of March 1987 quickly found a place in the 1988 Educational Reform Act, but he sees CTCs, grant-maintained schools and local management of schools as just stepping stones towards a fully privatized system. In such a system all schools would be private schools, and would be able to negotiate individual contracts of employment with teachers and other staff. The responsibility for education would be returned to the individual parent and family, who would receive an educational credit (voucher) for each child from the government. Wealthy parents could 'top-up' these credits and pay for any 'extras' that the school felt desirable, while those parents unwilling or unable to do so would condemn their children to a 'basic' education. Those with sufficient wealth would be given greater choice and would be able to buy privilege for their children, while the children of the poor would find their choices made for them. The cost would be greater social and ethnic segregation, less mutual understanding, and a reinforcement of the pre-existing social order of wealth and privilege.

What should be done?

The previous section has shown that the CTCs cannot engage in any meaningful way with most of the real and perceived problems and tasks that have been set for them. Although they will undoubtedly help those few children selected, they do not begin to tackle inner-city problems. Nor can they do very much to improve technical and vocational education, for the initiative is too small for that. Even the full twenty CTCs, working in isolation from other schools, cannot have any great impact on the roughly 7,000 secondary schools nation-wide. Moreover the co-operative inter-school method of curriculum change embodied in TVEI has shown itself to be a far more potent force for change than the establishment of isolated CTCs in antagonistic relation to other schools. In both of these areas the CTCs are a diversion which distracts attention from the issues rather than engage with them.

Again, the CTCs do offer a wider choice of school for the few children selected, but the initiative is too small for this to be significant nationally. Also, at Kingshurst a much larger number of children are now rejected than are granted their choice. The CTCs have, however, helped to legitimize inequality through the idea of choice. Indeed, it is only in privatization, selection and differentiation of provision according to the existing social order, that the CTCs actually begin to engage with the issues, and here they do so in a socially regressive way.

The CTCs have also been a very expensive experiment. It is correct for the supporters to point out that the approximately £50 million that has been contributed by British companies to CTCs is the largest ever private sector donation in support of a public education initiative, but the cost to the government has been three times this amount. This excludes the indirect costs in terms of central administration, the CTC Trust, advertising and so on, and the extra costs that LEAs have had to spend to counter and accommodate to CTCs in their areas. What is to be done about them?

The Labour Party has pledged that it will put the CTCs under LEA control, but it has not stated how this is to be done. Indeed, as there is already considerable diversity between the CTCs, there may be a need for different solutions for individual colleges. There have even been suggestions that some of the CTCs might become teacher-training schools, modelled on the teaching hospitals (Sutcliffe 1990). But the most important factor affecting the range of options is obviously the result of the next general election (due in 1991 or 1992) and the resulting colour of the next government.

The first possibility is that the Conservative Party will be returned for a fourth term of office. In this circumstance, it is probable that the planned twenty CTCs will gradually come into existence, followed by a watering down of the concept as DES funding is reduced to average LEA spending levels and industry spreads its support to a wider range of schools. While individual CTCs may still be able to attract additional funding from industry and commerce it is not to be expected that this will be large enough to sustain a dramatically different level of staffing or facilities once the CTCs are no longer in the headlines. If the CTC Trust is successful in its aim, the original CTC concept will be further diluted by including LEA-owned and controlled CTCs which will just receive a small amount of extra funding from industry.

The alternative scenario assumes a Labour victory in the 1991 or 1992 general election. The Shadow Secretary of State for Education, Jack Straw, has been fiercely critical of CTCs, and has stated that Labour would immediately cancel the programme and use the estimated £100 million released by this to repair and decorate existing LEA schools. The Labour Party has also stated that the CTCs are to be brought into the LEA system, but their status as private schools and the protection afforded to sponsors in the 1988 Education Reform Act do not make this straightforward. If Labour were returned to power with a large majority it might be possible for them to introduce retrospective legislation to nullify the guarantees given to sponsors in the 1988 Act, but this would be unpopular and provide a dangerous precedent. It would also take too much parliamentary time, when the new government would have far more important legislation to push through.

The alternative is to 'ease' the CTCs into closer co-operation with the LEAs through modification to the agreements made between the DES and each college. The crucial element here is that, while the CTCs are technically private schools, they are effectively dependent on the DES for almost all of their capital and running costs. If the government simply withdrew all funding it might be possible for some of the CTCs to cease to operate as CTCs and reopen as fee-paying and/or industry-supported schools or colleges. The possibility of turning them into private training colleges might be particularly attractive to some sponsors. However, any move into the fee-paying private sector would face legal and financial difficulties. The Labour Party would also not wish the previous government's investment to become part of the private sector. A more probably plan would be to modify the individual funding agreements between the DES and the colleges such that new conditions have to be met. Chief among these new conditions might be the inclusion of LEA and parent representatives on the governing bodies (teachers would still be ineligible due to charitable status) and full consultation on admissions with the relevant LEAs. Undoubtedly there would be a requirement that teachers are paid on the same salary scale and have the same conditions of service as other LEA teachers. It is probable that the catchment areas for admission would be increased, such that the effect of the CTC would be potentially less damaging to local comprehensive schools. These new conditions for the CTCs might also involve an obligation to share specialist scientific and technological facilities with nearby schools as has occurred in many TVEI projects. Both the wider catchment area and the obligation to share facilities would have the additional advantage of increased social mixing. The other major change that should be made is to the selection criteria, where we believe that random selection from amongst those who apply is likely to lead to the fairest outcome for all pupils. Diversity becomes unjust when one group has preferential access, and random selection ensures that parents cannot guarantee access for their own children (Walford 1990a: 120). It ensures that a diversity does not necessarily lead to a hierarchy of schools, for it is in the interests of parents to fight for the adequate support of state-maintained education as a whole, rather than for just one particular school.

The details of what new conditions would be imposed on CTCs if Labour were returned to power are uncertain. What is important is that the experience, facilities and good practice that are evident in some of the CTCs are not lost, and that the distracting, disrupting and counter-productive effects arising from the ideological manner in which they were established are overcome. This is best done by bringing the CTCs within the LEA framework such that *all* children in the area can benefit. Interestingly, The CTC Kingshurst affirms its Mission Statement that it 'remains within the State education system'. This does not reflect its political origin or its current legal status, but may augur well for its eventual integration within a system of schooling under local democratic control where the benefits from this initiative could find their fullest expression.

References

Ashworth, John, Papps, Ivy and Thomas, Barry (1988). *Increased Parental Choice?* London, Institute of Economic Affairs.

Association of Metropolitan Authorities (1987). *City Technology Colleges: A Speculative Investment.* London, AMA.

Ball, Stephen J. (1988). 'A comprehensive school in a pluralist world – division and inequalities'. In Bernadette O'Keeffe (ed.) *Schools for Tomorrow.* Lewes, Falmer.

Bernstein, Basil (1970). 'Education cannot compensate for society'. *New Society*, 387, February.

Biddle, Denise (1985). *History of Kingshurst.* Solihull, Solihull Metropolitan Borough Council/Manpower Services Commission.

Birmingham City Council (1990). *Entry to Grammar Schools at 11 Years of Age 1990.* Birmingham Education Committee.

Bowcott, O. (1983). 'School plan biased, say heads', *Birmingham Post*, 20 September.

Brown, M., Chope, C., Fallon, M., Forsyth, M., Hamilton, N., Howarth, G., Jones, R., Leigh, E., Lilley, P., Maude, F., Portillo, M., Rumbold, A., and Twinn, I. (1985). *No Turning Back.* London, Conservative Political Centre.

Brown, M., Chope, C., Fallon, M., Forth, E., Forsyth, M., Hamilton, N., Howarth, G., Jones, R., Leigh, E., Lilley, P., Portillo, M., and Twinn, I. (1986). *Save Our Schools.* London, Conservative Political Centre.

Burgess, Robert G. (1983). *Experiencing Comprehensive Education: A Study of Bishop McGregor School.* London, Methuen.

—— (1987). 'Studying and restudying Bishop McGregor School'. In Geoffrey Walford (ed.) *Doing Sociology of Education*. Lewes, Falmer.

Burn, John and Hart, Colin (1988). *The Crisis in Religious Education*. London, Educational Research Trust.

Carvel, John and Boseley, Sarah (1986). 'Inner city colleges launched by Baker'. *The Guardian*, 8 October, 1.

Conniff, Caroline (1989). 'CTC schools sacrificed to god of privatization'. *Times Educational Supplement*, 7 April.

Cooper, Bruce (1987). *Magnet Schools*. London, Institute of Economic Affairs.

Cowie, Helen and Rudduck, Jean (1988a). *Co-Operative Group Work: An Overview*. London, BP International Limited.

—— (1988b). *School and Classroom Studies*. London, BP International Limited.

Cox, Caroline (1985). 'Many attractions of the magnet'. *Times Educational Supplement*, 15 March.

Cox, C.B. and Dyson, A. (eds) (1971). *Black Papers on Education 1–3*. London, Davis-Poynter.

Cox, C.B. and Boyson, Rhodes (eds) (1975). *Black Paper 4*. London, Dent.

—— (eds) (1977) *Black Paper 1977*. London, Temple Smith/The Adam Smith Institute.

Davies, Bernard (1986). *Threatening Youth. Towards a National Youth Policy*. Milton Keynes, Open University Press.

Dennison, S.R. (1984). *Choice in Education*, Hobart Paperback 19. London, Institute of Economic Affairs.

Department of Education and Science (1986). *City Technology Colleges. A New Choice of School*. London, DES.

—— (1989a). *Statistics of Schools in England – January 1988*. Statistical Bulletin 8/89. London, DES.

—— (1989b). *Survey of Information Technology in Schools*. Statistical Bulletin 10/89. London, DES.

Dobson, Ken (1989). 'Suffolk Co-Ordinated Science – results of the first pilot phase'. *Change in Focus: Towards a Better Science*, No. 3, Spring.

Edwards, Tony, Fitz, John and Whitty, Geoff (1989). *The State and Private Education. An Evaluation of the Assisted Places Scheme*. Lewes, Falmer.

Edwards, Tony, Gewirtz, Sharon and Whitty, Geoff (1991). From Assisted Places to City Technology Colleges. In Geoffrey Walford (ed.) *Private Schooling: Tradition, Change and Diversity*. London, Paul Chapman.

Giddens, Anthony (1985). *The Nation-State and Violence*. Oxford, Polity.

Griggs, Clive (1985). *Private Education*. Lewes, Falmer.

Hadfield, Greg (1989). 'Stars line up with Baker to launch academy of fame'. *Sunday Times*, 29 January.

Hargreaves, David (1967). *Social Relations in a Secondary School*. London, Routledge & Kegan Paul.

Heron, Elizabeth (1989). 'New CTC will have one foot in Europe'. *Times Educational Supplement*, 31 March.

Humphrey, Colin (1983). *Structure of Secondary Education: Reintroduction of Selective Schools* (1st report). Report of the Director of Education, Metropolitan Borough of Solihull, 21 September.

—— (1984). *Structure of Secondary Education: Selection and Standards*. (2nd report). Report of Director of Education, Metropolitan Borough of Solihull, 29 February.

—— (1988). *Financial Autonomy in Solihull*. London, Institute of Economic Affairs.

Humphrey, Colin and Thomas, Hywel (1986). 'Delegating to schools', *Education*, 12, 513–14.

Kingman Report (1988). *Report of the Committee of Inquiry into the Teaching of English Language*. London, HMSO.

Labour Research (1988). 'City Technology Colleges – sponsoring an elite', *Labour Research*, 77, 11, 7–9.

Lacey, Colin (1970). *Hightown Grammar*. Manchester, Manchester University Press.

McCulloch, Gary (1989). *The Secondary Technical School: A Usable Past?* Lewes, Falmer.

Makins, Virginia (1989). 'Transforming old ideas into new technology', *Times Educational Supplement*, 15 September.

Mannheim, Karl (1960). *Ideology and Utopia*. London, Routledge & Kegan Paul.

Marx, Karl and Engels, Friedrich (1939). *The German Ideology*. London, International Publishers.

Mayo, Elton (1933). *The Human Problems of an Industrial Civilization*. New York, Macmillan.

Measor, Lynda and Woods, Peter (1984). *Changing Schools: Pupil Perspectives on Transfer to a Comprehensive School*. Milton Keynes, Open University Press.

Merton, Robert K. (1968). *Social Theory and Social Structure*. New York, Free Press.

Metz, Mary Haywood (1986). *Different by Design. The Context and Character of Three Magnet Schools*. London, Routledge & Kegan Paul.

Morrell, Frances (1989). *Children of the Future*. London, Hogarth Press.

Moss, Stephen (1989). *An investigation into the links between education and industry in the West Midlands*. Unpublished MSc dissertation, Aston University.

Nash, Ian (1988). 'CTCs forced to alter tack', *Times Educational Supplement*, 17 June, 1.

O'Connor, Maureen (1989). 'Dobson's choice pays off', *The Guardian*, 28 February.

Official Guide (1987). *Solihull Metropolitan Borough Council Official Guide*. Solihull.

Perkin, Harold (1989). *The Rise of Professional Society. England since 1880*. London, Routledge.

Phillips, Susan (1989). *The impact of the City Technology College on local businesses*. Unpublished MBA dissertation, Aston University.

Pollard, Andrew, Purvis, June and Walford, Geoffrey (eds) (1988). *Education, Training and the New Vocationalism: Experience and Policy*. Milton Keynes, Open University Press.

Quicke, John (1988). 'The New Right and education', *British Journal of Educational Studies*, 36, 1, 5–20.

Reader, David. (1979). 'A recurring debate: education and industry'. In Gerald Bernbaum (ed.) *Schooling in Decline*. London, Macmillan.

Regan, David (1990). *City Technology Colleges: Potentialities and Perils*. London, Centre for Policy Studies.

Royal Society for the Arts (1983). *Education for Capability*. London, RSA.

Science and Technology Regional Organization (1987). *Education for Enterprise: The Power Station Game*. London, SATRO.

Sexton, Stuart (1977). 'Evolution by choice'. In C.B. Cox and Rhodes Boyson (eds) *Black Paper 1977*. London, Temple Smith.

—— (1987). *Our Schools – A Radical Policy*. London, Institute of Economic Affairs.

Simon, Brian (1988). *Bending the Rules*. London, Lawrence & Wishart.

Slater, Sidney M. (1987). 'Delivering the goods. Education and industry: A partnership in action'. *School Organization*, 7, 1, 35–38.

Slater, Sidney (1988a). 'Industrial links'. In David Warwick (ed.) *Teaching and Learning through Modules*. Oxford, Blackwell.

—— (1988b). 'Appraising teachers'. In Les Bell (ed.) *Appraising Teachers in School: A Practical Guide*. London, Routledge.

Slater, Sidney and Hanley, Terry (1989). 'An active partnership'. In David Warwick (ed.) *Linking Schools and Industry*. Oxford, Blackwell.

Slavin, R. (1987). *Learning to Co-operate: Co-operating to Learn*. New York, Plenum.

Sutcliffe, Jeremy (1990). 'Heresy may pave the path to power', *Times Educational Supplement*, 3 August.

Taylor, Cyril (1986). *Employment Examined: The Right Approach to More Jobs*. London, Centre for Policy Studies.

Thomas, Hywel, Kirkpatrick, Gordon and Nicholson, Elizabeth (1989). *Financial Delegation and the Local Management of Schools*. Poole, Cassell.

Toogood, Philip (1984). *The Head's Tale*. London, Dialogue Publications.

Vulliamy, Edward (1987). 'Industrialists attack city colleges', *The Guardian*, 16 March, 1.

Walford, Geoffrey (1986). *Life in Public Schools*. London, Methuen.

—— (1987a). 'How dependent is the independent sector?', *Oxford Review of Education*, 13, 3, 275–96.

—— (1987b). 'Research role conflicts and compromises in public schools'. In Geoffrey Walford (ed.) *Doing Sociology of Education*. Lewes, Falmer.

—— (1990a). *Privatization and Privilege in Education*. London, Routledge.

—— (1990b). 'Developing choice in British education', *Compare*, 20, 1, 67–81.

—— (1990c). 'The 1988 Education Reform Act for England and Wales: paths to privatization', *Educational Policy*, 4, 2, 127–44.

—— (1991a). 'Investigating the City Technology College, Kingshurst'. In Geoffrey Walford (ed.) *Doing Educational Research*. London, Routledge.

—— (1991b). 'The reluctant private sector: of small schools, people and politics'. In Geoffrey Walford (ed.) *Private Schooling: Tradition, Change and Diversity*. London, Paul Chapman.

—— (ed.) (1991c). *Private Schooling: Tradition. Change and Diversity*. London, Paul Chapman.

Walford, Geoffrey and Jones, Siân (1986). 'The Solihull adventure: an attempt to reintroduce selective schooling', *Journal of Education Policy*, 1, 3, 239–53.

Walford, Geoffrey, Purvis, June and Pollard, Andrew (1988). 'Ethnography, policy and the emergence of the new vocationalism'. In Andrew Pollard, June Purvis and Geoffrey Walford (eds) *Education, Training and the New Vocationalism: Experience and Policy*. Milton Keynes, Open University Press.

Whitty, Geoff, Edwards, Tony and Gewirtz, Sharon (forthcoming) *City Technology Colleges: A New Choice of School?*

Wiener, Martin J. (1981). *English Culture and the Decline of the Industrial Spirit 1850–1980*. Cambridge, Cambridge University Press.

Index

Carlisle, M., 5, 6
Carvel, J., 10
Castle Bromwich, 22–4, 104, 105
catalyst, 157–8
catchment area, 21, 23, 104–7,
    133
Centre for Policy Studies, 8
Certificate of Pre-Vocational
    Education, 33
Chapeltown, 2
Chelmsley Wood, 23
Cincinatti, 30
City College for the Technology
    of the Arts, 19, 140, 151
City Technology Colleges Trust,
    15, 18, 167
Cockshut Hill School, 28, 132–4
Coleshill School, 117, 141
computers, 50, 67–9, 71, 74, 90,
    92–4
Conniff, C., 151
Conservative Party, 1, 16, 167
Cooper, B., 17
Corby CTC, 148
Cowie, H., 78, 82
Cox, C., 7, 17, 148
Cox, C.B., 4
Croydon, 19, 147, 149, 150
Culey Green School, 25, 40, 132,
    136
curriculum, 12, 72–8, 154–5

Dartford, 19, 147, 149
Davies, B., 7
Davy Corporation, 18
Dennison, S.R., 7
Derby CTC, 148, 152
Dicken, A., 148
direct grant schools, 5
Director of Administration and
    Finance, 58, 64, 110
Dixons, 16, 17, 147
Djanogly, H., 17, 147
Djanogly College, 147

Dobson, K., 76
Downs School, 19, 150
Dunn, R., 9, 35, 37
Dyson, A., 4

economic awareness, 60, 76–7
Edwards, T., 5, 6, 87, 96, 112,
    113, 116, 121
Ellis, M., 35
Emmanuel College, 147, 148
employers, 141–6
Engels, F., 159
English, 74–5, 79
enrichments, 73, 77–8
equipment, 70–72
ethnicity, 106, 110
expectations, 88–91

Fitz, J., 5, 6, 87, 96, 112, 113, 116
freedom, 97–100
funding, 63–4
funding agreement, 15, 61

Gateshead, 19, 147, 148
Gewirtz, S., 121
Giddens, A., 159
Glasgow CTC, 148
grammar schools, 27, 28, 34, 55,
    107, 121, 133
grant maintained schools, 4, 139–40
Greenleaf Planters, 151
Griggs, C., 6
group work, 79–82, 83–4, 96

Haberdashers' Aske's Hatcham
    Schools, 19, 147, 149
Hadfield, G., 151
Hall, J., 18
Handsworth, 2, 163
Hanley, T., 30
Hanson plc, 16, 17, 38, 63, 141,
    145, 147
Hargreaves, D.H., 120
Harris, Sir P., 16, 149, 150